No Beard or Bowtie Required
Cocktails for the Craft-Curious

No Beard or Bowtie Required: Cocktails for the Craft-Curious

ISBN 13 (print): 978-1-937513-95-5
First edition
Published by http://www.cooperativepress.com

Text ©2021 Tim Harnett
Photos ©2021 Victoria Stanbridge
Editor: Ilona Westfall
Cover art: Kymm Bang

Every effort has been made to ensure that all the information in this book is accurate at the time of publication; however, Cooperative Press neither endorses nor guarantees the content of external links referenced in this book.

If you have questions or comments about this book, or need information about licensing, custom editions, special sales, or academic/corporate purchases, please contact Cooperative Press: info@cooperativepress.com or 10252 Berea Rd, Cleveland, Ohio 44102 USA

No part of this book may be reproduced in any form, except brief excerpts for the purpose of review, without prior written permission of the publisher. Thank you for respecting our copyright.

No Beard or Bowtie Required
Cocktails for the Craft-Curious*

Cooperative Press
Cleveland, Ohio

(*Warning: This book contains coarse language and a good deal of smugness.)

Dedicated to Carol,
My rock and designated driver for 30 years,
And to all the Cleveland bartenders that taught me what I know

Table of Contents

Foreword   8

Chapter 1: Raising your Spirits   11

Chapter 2: The Bedfellows of Booze   23
- Practice Round 1: The Classic Martini   31
- Practice Round 2: The Margarita   33
- Practice Round 3: The Classic Daiquiri   35
- Practice Round 4: The Manhattan   35

Chapter 3: Under the Influence   36
- Mai Tai   39
- Fairytale of Bourbon County   41
- The Old Brooklyn   41
- The Oswald Cobblerpot   43
- Tropical Turbulence   45
- Suffering Diablo   45
- Polynesian 75   47
- Motobecane   47

Chapter 4: Highballs, Elevated to Collins   48
- Serpent and the Rainbow   51
- Elizabeth, My Dear   51
- Lux Interior   53
- The Suffering Soda Jerk   55
- American Splendor   55
- Dead Man's Curve Revisited   57

Chapter 5: Under the Gin-fluence   58
- Hulk Smash   61
- Reverse Flash Smash   61
- Babylon-a-Go-Go   63
- Your Mother was a Hamster   63
- Farewell, Solenya   65
- Domo Arigato, Mr. Sfumato   65
- Pride, Prejudice & Headhunters   67
- Sonic Reducer   67
- Dutch Feast   68

Chapter 6: Rumbullion   70
- The Careless Navigator   73
- Wrong 'Em, Boyo   73
- Rhu Morgue   75
- French 71   75
- Queen Be   77
- Trinidad Shakedown   77
- Express Kundalini   79
- Johnny Mo   79
- Kill Devil Blues   81
- Highway 78 Revisited   81
- Mermaid Smiled   82
- The Winter Soldier   82
- Timm's Cup #3   83
- Krakoa   83

Chapter 7: El Efecto Tequila — 84

- Electric Eel — 87
- Alvin Purple — 87
- The Alpine Standoff — 89
- Repo Man — 89
- Nick the Bubble — 91
- Johnny Nash — 91
- Thunder Buddies — 93
- There Will be Blood — 93
- Quemando tu Casa — 94
- The Deer Hunter — 94
- Mirador Hotel — 97
- Praying Mantis — 97

Chapter 8: Whiskey Rebellion — 98

- Teddy Roosevelt's Fox — 101
- The Sarah Winchester — 101
- The Rye-cycle Thief — 102
- Roman Holiday — 102
- Pushin' Up Daisies — 103
- Nick Knox — 103
- Bigallet Trouble in Little China-China — 105
- Scotch Bonnet — 105
- Bomb City USA — 106
- Alternating Currant — 106
- High Noon — 107
- Danny Greene — 107
- Blizzard of 77 — 109
- Grave Disorder — 109
- The White Queen — 111
- Concerto Macabro (aka Hangover Square) — 111
- Let Me Stare into those Mince Pies — 112

Chapter 9: Polynesian Remedies — 114

- Gorilla Panic!!! — 116
- Five-Finger Death Punsch — 117
- Stiv's Tomb #2 — 117
- Inu Poni — 119
- Tropic Thunder — 119
- Cheetah Chrome — 121
- Pouli Kalikimaka — 121
- Kumu Hula — 123
- Gaelic Grog — 123
- Kaiser Kai — 125

Chapter 10: Stranger Than Paradise — 126

- An Italian Werewolf in Norway — 129
- Voice of the Beehive — 129
- Space Heater — 130
- Tea - Mr. Brownstone — 130
- Coffee - A Cold Day in Hell — 130
- Crash and Burn — 131
- A Date with Elvis — 133
- Bar Car on the Orient Express — 133
- Pear Ubu — 135
- Poison Ivy — 135
- Pagan's Progress — 137
- Stockholm Syndrome — 137
- Halo Effect — 138

Appendix — 139

Foreword

Right now I make a living as a cocktail bartender. Unlike most of my male colleagues in the industry, my face remains beard free. And the skill to tie a bowtie still evades me. My contemporaries also hustle harder, as they're usually in their 20s and 30s while I'm courting 52. But I digress, and am really jumping too far ahead in my story.

The paths to professional craft cocktailing vary a bit from one barkeep's tale to the next. But in my experience, it's usually younger people who joined the industry fresh out of college. They discovered their acumen for mixology, then elevated their craft and reputation to admirable heights before even hitting 30. Many won awards, opened bars, wrote books. Many grew beards and learned to tie bowties.

I started as a misguided drunk.

My story does begin with the college part, but decades delayed me from life behind the bar. I entered legal drinking age in 1990 as a Junior at Bowling Green State University. Then, I shrugged off the cheap 12-packs and poor spirits of adolescence purchasing party beverages for my underage student friends. Considering the criminality of buying for multiple minors each week, using their change to buy myself a new kind of craft beer was surely no further test of my moral fabric.

That's where it all began. Sure, the effects of ethanol are basically the same at any price tag. But once you discover you can also savor every sip of your intoxicants, there's really no returning to cheap swill. Upon graduation in 1991, I swore ongoing allegiance to craft beer and spirits until death.

Soul-crushing corporate jobs consumed the following 25 years. My degree would have better served me as a drink coaster. And each step up the corporate ladder subtracted a degree of happiness. But these career missteps allowed me to mingle with a growing universe of craft spirits. Seemingly interminable days in cubicles often ended with sublime blends of bitters, amaros, and vermouths.

This brush fire was fueled by an ongoing subscription to Imbibe Magazine, a biblically important periodical for anyone that respects what they put in a glass. While obsessively fascinating, my first few issues frustrated me with recipes calling for spirits I didn't have: Aromatized wines, eclectic bitters, unusual cordials. To rectify this, I resolved to obtain a new bottle of spirit with each new issue.

By 2010, our Cleveland home swelled with two full bars hemorrhaging with a vast array of spirits. Visiting industry friends guided us along the way, helping select proper bar tools and glassware, and also to hone correct stirring and shaking techniques. So while drinking quite heavily to cope with serving my daily sentence in a cubicle, a professional grade bartender emerged from the wreckage. This took about five years.

Almost inevitably I decided to explore a paying career in mixology. Still chained to the desk, I enjoyed the most ample salary of my life, great benefits, and exceptional retirement perks. But I also suffered three to four hangovers per work week simply to enjoy a few hours of escape. Just to test the waters, I moonlighted once a week as a tiki mixologist at a local rum distillery starting in 2015.

These few evening hours behind the bar convinced me that I suffered "imposter syndrome" sitting at a desk. A close friend in the bar industry described this malady as the persistent sensation of being a fraud in one's profession, no matter how lasting and successful this career might prove to be. It can further lead to thoughts of pretty dark alternatives to continuing career dissatisfaction.

My tolerance for corporate life died in the summer of 2016. Perhaps serendipitously, a close friend launched what became Cleveland's hottest craft cocktail bar, high atop the prestigious downtown Hilton Hotel. This baptism of fire prepared me for ongoing opportunities to lead the drink program at other Cleveland destination bars. The present day has brought me full circle back to tiki bartending — what I consider the true acid test of craft cocktailing skill.

For full disclosure, imposter syndrome tends to stick. It stays with me despite five years of growth and success in the bar industry. This book represents one way of exorcising that demon. It also aims to show you the potential for amazing cocktails in the comfort of home. Perhaps it will also show you where budding cocktail creativity can take you (maybe even rescue you from a news story concluding with "before turning the gun on himself").

The chapters that follow mimic my path to career bartending. You'll start with that humbling learning stage. You'll then get deeper into flavor and spirit combinations that unfolded across a decade of shaking and stirring.

The big point to drive home is that the bespoke waistcoat, bowtie, and carefully groomed facial hair are simply the wrapping for many gifted cocktailers, not a requirement*.

---

*Quick side note — the book title in no way took inspiration from Phil Collins' No Jacket Required. Who or what the hell is "Sussudio"? Plus, you ruined Genesis. Get stuffed, Phil.

Chapter 1: Raising your Spirits

I possessed an infantile knowledge of cocktailing at the start. While it's something I believe most everyone can do, it does take some commitment to soak up the minimum knowledge and the skills. Hell, I once relied on note cards to differentiate Manhattans from Old Fashioneds for months (much less execute them).

Many mixologist authors whom I admire wrote pretty exhaustive chapters on tools and technique. While you can never learn too much when it comes to bartending, I want to give you what I consider just enough to be dangerous. Guerilla level, if you will. Revolutions are normally funded on small budgets after all.

So this chapter will lay out some basic spirits you should have at the ready, additional cocktail components, and the minimum tools you'll need. These recommendations stem from my personal experiences and advice from the better minds that taught me what I know.

Should you feel you're well equipped when it comes to tools and tipples, I won't judge if you jump to the recipes in the next chapter. Consider this paragraph the "skip intro" button when you're binging several seasons of Boardwalk Empire.

High Proof Spirits

These include any distilled spirits at 42 proof/21% alcohol by volume. You balance this more potent base with other ingredients in any cocktail, which often have lower strengths and different flavors that balance out the finished concoction.

Spirits begin as a fermented lower proof liquid. Distillers call these "distiller's beer" when made using grains, or "distiller's wine" when made from grapes or other fruits. Distilling heats up these lower proof liquids into vapors. The water separates from the alcohol vapors, which are then condensed back into a higher-strength liquid.

Generally speaking, "higher shelf" spirits in any category usually offer the best flavor. Stores display the lowest cost (and consequently worst tasting spirits) on the bottom shelf. Plenty of solid spirits sit on the middle shelves. These just require a little research to find out which ones render the best cocktail at the most reasonable price.

The rest of this chapter lays out some recommendations for good, affordable spirits and other staple ingredients that enable you to make a range of classic cocktails at any given time. Bear in mind that the chapters to follow stipulate ingredients that, while easily obtainable, are often more eclectic and specific to single cocktail recipes.

Let's start with the high proof spirit that you don't need.

Vodka: Also known as grain neutral spirit or "GNS," it's colorless and, for all intents and purposes, without aroma or flavor. Cocktailing is about creating sublimely flavorful drinks. You will not accomplish this with a tasteless spirit, nor the artificially-flavored versions that horde up valuable shelf space at your local spirits store. Any trace of flavor depends on the grain or fruit from which the spirit is made. These usually include corn, other grains, or even grapes. Potatoes are oddly quite rare, but have you ever tasted a raw potato? Blech.

Should you default to Moscow Mules at any given bar, you should probably take this book straight to the used book shop for the $1.25 that it might garner. But mind you, vodka's versatility much improves if you naturally infuse it with citrus peels, herbs, spices, or other botanicals. Some recipes in this book will call for infused vodka, though I confess these spawned from pressures to offer vodka drinks at certain bars on my resume.

If you must have vodka, Ketel One or Belvedere are reputable spirits. But hell, if you want to run a lemonade stand that only sells water, be my guest.

Gin

And now, what you do need.

Gin: Much to my point on infusions, craft cocktail bartenders jokingly deem gin "the first flavored vodka." To release this neutral spirit from its cocoon of blandness, botanicals like herbs, citrus peels, and other floral plants are combined with it. Any gin must feature juniper as the most prominent botanical and include at least two other plants in the mix. Gins such as Death's Door use the minimum three, while more complex gins like Monkey 47 use, well, 47.

Distillers employ one of three methods to marry botanicals with the neutral spirit. Gin lovers usually attribute the "gin basket" to exceptionally flavorful gins. During distillation, gin vapors pass through this porous vessel and absorb the botanical flavors. Gin producers can also make good spirits by steeping the botanicals in the distiller's beer or wine before distillation. The final method called "compounding" simply blends separately-distilled liquid botanicals into high proof neutral spirit. While good compounded gins exist, this method typically produces the least expensive and less well-regarded gins.

Most people equate any gin with the London Dry style that's most commonly made. Many gins made in the United States do resemble these ancestors in many ways, but fall into the "New Western" category due to their common reliance on less juniper. Earlier styles of gin including Dutch Genever and "Old Tom" typically lean sweeter. Some distillers also barrel age gins to impart flavors from the previously-aged spirit, be it bourbon, rye, even red or white wine.

Needless to say, your gin compliment can offer a wider array of flavors than one might realize. Good home bars keep one or two quality London Dry brands handy, and perhaps an Old Tom such as Anchor or Hayman's. Early cocktail bars relied heavily upon Old Tom, so you might consider it a matter of cocktailing heritage to include one in your own home bar.

And don't let bad adolescent experiences with grandpa's dusty bottle of Seagram's deter you from a splendid cocktail spirit. Gin provides a vast array of flavors with which to experiment, from the dry, assertive Tanqueray to the sweet, rosy notes of Nolet's Silver.

Tequila & Mezcal

Many perceive tequila as a rough spirit that unlocks Mr. Hyde from their psyche. No matter your perception, today this Mexican agave distillate enjoys a craft renaissance unlike any other. Tequila distillers only use the Weber blue variety of agave, which is grown in five Mexican states with Jalisco being at its epicenter.

Tequila commonly gives you a sweeter base to build upon, often with a slight tinge of pepper. The climate conditions, harvesting, baking and distilling practices where it's made impart variations on these flavors. If bottled directly after distillation, producers usually call this "silver" or "blanco."

Most distillers also age tequila, commonly in used American whiskey barrels, and to a lesser extent in barrels used for wine or other spirits. Some silver tequilas spend a short period in barrels to soften their flavor. "Reposado" or "rested" tequila spends anywhere up to a year in barrels, which gives it a more oaky flavor and straw color.

Tequila lovers more often crave spirits aged longer. "Anejo" tequila ages longer than reposado, typically for at least two years. "Extra anejo" denotes tequila aged for three years or more. These sweeter, more robust, and coveted spirits usually wear the higher price tags of the fine whiskies that they often mimic.

Whether aged or not, only purchase 100% agave tequilas. Distillers can use as little as 51% agave spirit and fill the balance with cheaper neutral spirits or sweeteners. These "mixto" tequilas cost as much as other 100% agave spirits on the same shelf, but pale in flavor and quality. "Gold" is also best avoided as it typically gains its shade from caramel coloring.

Good pure-agave tequila can be obtained even in restrictive liquor control states like Ohio. This list cites tequilas you can commonly obtain in any state at a very reasonable cost:

- Espolon - Silver and Reposado
- Altos - Silver, Reposado and Anejo
- Cazadores - Silver up to Extra Anejo
- El Jimador - Silver and Reposado
- Mi Campo - Silver and Reposado

Mezcal resembles tequila mainly in its use of agave, though this spirit can be made with several more and often much rarer plant strains. Mezcal producers bake their agave hearts using open smoke, giving the final spirit a very smoky flavor. More than a half-ounce of Mezcal can overpower the other elements in a cocktail with smoke flavor. So "Mezcal-forward" mixtures are quite uncommon.

More mezcals from small craft producers appear in the U.S. each year. "Joven" or young (unaged) mezcals tend to dominate the meager shelf space they get. But you will see occasional reposado and anejo versions. Mezcal comes from nearly double the number of tequila-producing states. But as smoky spirit fans prove more rarified, tequila demands a much stronger presence than its close cousin.

Good and accessible mezcal producers include Del Maguey (Vida being most affordable) and Ilegal. Mezcals do cost a bit more than other spirits because artisanal distillers dominate this category. Monte Alban is an exception, but it sits on the bottom shelf for all the reasons that "bottom shelf" is a pejorative term. This, or any other bottle containing a worm, should instead preserve said organism with formaldehyde, which more than likely tastes better.

Rum

Several sub-styles fall under the rum umbrella. Originating in the Caribbean islands, distillers either make rum from the extractions of sugar cane plants, or from molasses — the dark, thick, and intensely sweet by-product of sugar refining. Molasses naturally produces sweeter rum. Conversely, the straight cane or "agricole" (agricultural) rums are more funky, earthy, and vegetal. You will typically see the French spelling "Rhum" on agricole bottles, as Martinique most commonly produces this style.

Rum played a pivotal role in early cocktailing. During Prohibition, sealed Carribean rum offered a safe alternative to unsafe, tampered spirits like bathtub gin. Meanwhile, Cuba led the rum cocktail charge, creating timeless classics like the daiquiri. Rum's importance and versatility in the cocktail world cannot be overstated.

Consider in particular that multiple blends of rum from different regions can be combined in a single cocktail with exquisite results. No other spirit really offers this creative palette. You don't expect to see cocktails with multiple types of gin or whiskey, which the country preferred before and after Prohibition. As is the case with vodka, flavored varieties of rum largely hold no merit and waste valuable shelf space both at spirit stores and in bars. Some craft distillers do produce naturally-infused pineapple rums, recognizing this heritage tradition from the Caribbean. Tiki Lovers, Plantation, and Maggie's Farm make stellar pineapple rums.

Also, be cautious assuming what rum bottle labeling implies. A number on the label doesn't necessarily indicate the rum's age. Likewise, terms like "dark" may not mean the rum gets its darkness from barrel aging. Good rum distillers very explicitly spell out any age statement, production methods, and origins of the rum(s) in the bottle.

Rum clearly holds a dear place to me. So rather than wax on about it, here's a quick summary of some basic styles and recommendations for good, affordable bottles:

- **Silver, white, or blanco rum:** Often the most affordable, silver rum is typically unaged. Some aged examples exist, but these are filtered to remove color. My bar consistently stocks Plantation 3 Star, Bounty White, and Angostura White Oak.
- **Gold rum:** Like the name implies, gold rum should have a pale yellow color from barrel resting. Avoid mass-market examples and seek out Bounty Gold or Rum Bar Gold.
- **Dark rum:** Proper dark rum gains its brown hue and softer sweetness from barrel-aging, quite commonly in used American bourbon barrels. Beware of caramel-colored dark rum. Appleton Estate, Plantation Dark and Mount Gay Eclipse are my go-to dark rums and very affordable.
- **Spiced rum:** Rum geeks usually frown on this category, and rightfully so, because most mass-produced examples are artificially flavored and colored. Given the chance, I'd wipe Captain Morgan from the planet. Proper spiced rums infuse natural spices like cinnamon, allspice, star anise, and orange peel. Use Chairman's Reserve, Bounty, and Lemon Hart Blackpool spiced rums without reservation.
- **Agricole/Cachaca:** Both of these styles are cane spirits and impart a more funky, grassy flavor than molasses-based rums. Agricoles hail from Martinique. Cachaca enjoys the title of Brazil's native spirit. I recommend Clement and Rhum J.M agricole and Avua Cachaca. Leblon or 51 Cachaca might be more easily available.
- **Blackstrap rum:** Fewer producers make this style. But its deep, dark molasses color and flavor deserve special attention. It's strong, sweet flavor makes a huge impact in cocktails. Cruzan makes a solid blackstrap rum in very affordable liter bottles.

I could spiral off on a tangent about more styles and origins of rum like Solera, but in my mind, most of these are sipping rums that don't commonly make their way into cocktails. But even high-age statement rums come at less cost than other high-age spirits. Therefore you can use more exquisite rums in daiquiris or other cocktails without cringing at the price.

Whisk(e)y

Like rum, whiskey demands entire books to adequately cover its history and breadth of flavors. But unlike rum, many devotees consider shaken whiskey cocktails blasphemous, citing that shaking it will "bruise" it. Frankly, I've never understood what this myth means and have enjoyed disproving it for years.

Whiskies include spirits made from grains like corn, wheat, rye, barley, and malt. Blends of these grains comprise the spirit's "mashbill" and determine its style and flavor. The method and proof to which whiskies are distilled distinguishes them from other spirits made with the same grains. Most whiskies also age in barrels in order to give it more character and soften its rough young flavors.

Let's stroll through the key styles and flavors, along with good, inexpensive brands.

Bourbon: This is America's whiskey. The surprising misconception I'd often hear is that all whiskies are bourbons, when the opposite is plainly true. Bourbon can be made in any of the 48 continental U.S. states, no matter what Kentuckians tell you. To be called bourbon, corn must comprise at least 51% of the mashbill. It must also age in new American oak barrels, but for no prescribed amount of time.

Corn dominates most bourbon mashbills, so you can usually expect a sweeter spirit. "Wheated" bourbons like Maker's Mark also gain additional sweetness. Other grains like rye will temper the sweet side. My preferred, affordable mixing bourbons include Russell's Reserve, the Old Forester lineup, and Buffalo Trace.

Rye: You probably twigged that rye makes up the bulk of a rye whiskey mashbill. This American whiskey bites a little more sharply with a spicier grain character. This holds especially true for the popular "95/5" ryes that include only 5% of another grain. Ryes appeal to those with distaste for bourbon sweetness; good ryes like Michter's, Sazerac, Templeton, and Rittenhouse will make a less sweet Manhattan and better please those drinkers.

Scotch: Seems pretty obvious but this spirit comes from Scotland. When I worked at a distillery, one of those baffling questions I'd get was "do you guys make a Scotch?" Well, unless a sorcerer magically transported the property to Scotland, no. It must take a Scotch snob to know this, and also that the Scots spell it "whisky."

Many books devote fully to Scotch, and deservedly so. Five regions of Scotland make superb and distinct whisky that usually exceeds stringent style parameters. All are made with grains and/or malt, must barrel age for at least three years (usually many more), and must be distilled at least twice (sometimes up to 20 times). Distillers commonly use bourbon barrels.

Some examples of Scotch use traditions that deter many people from the entire category. Principal among these are peat, which is sometimes used to smoke Scotch malt. This gives the final spirit an astringent taste that only appeals to certain palates. Seaside distilleries also produce whisky that has a strong tinge of iodine. Again, a very acquired taste. Bartenders mainly use these as an aromatic glass rinse rather than a primary ingredient in cocktails.

Scotch comes either as single-malt or the single distillate of one producer, or as blends. Many single malts comprise blended Scotch. Single malts really fall into the neat whisky drinker's court, not just because their distinct flavors would be lost in cocktails, but also because of their higher cost. But good, inexpensive single malts like Speyburn better fit in the mixing realm. For better availability and mixing, steer towards good blends like Monkey Shoulder and The Famous Grouse.

Irish Whiskey: Only until recently has this sleeper category of whiskey re-emerged. Prohibition nearly destroyed the category by wiping out exports, leaving only recognizable brands like Jameson and Bushmills in its wake. Today, smaller regional distillers produce some outstanding and affordable whiskies that are wonderful for mixed drinks.

Irish whiskey shares many parallels with Scotch as far as mashbills and distillation. Few use peat, but some are single malts and some are blends. But by and large Irish whiskey costs less than Scotch. If using bigger brands, the non-flagship examples like Jameson Black Barrel have more character. I'd suggest hunting for Sexton, Slane, and Teeling Irish whiskies. These gain sublime flavors from secondary aging in casks used previously for spirits like rum and sherry.

Canadian whiskey: Honestly I only include this category as a courtesy to a wonderful country. The bulk of their whiskies belong on the back bars of seedy locals that probably haven't paid for their liquor license in years. Should I ever need to emigrate, I do hope Canada's immigration department does not find this book.

Canada makes most of its whiskey with rye, but can legally add caramel coloring and nearly over 9% imported spirit. Generally I'd advise avoiding the large-scale brands that come from Windsor. If you want any compliment of Canada in your bar, seek out the smaller craft gems like Pike Creek or Gooderham & Worts Four Grain. Oddly some expensive American brands like Whistle Pig also currently come from Canadian distilleries.

Brandies & Cordials & Amari & Vermouth

Brandy: Much beloved as a classic cocktail staple in the western world, brandy was not just the favorite tipple of Winston Churchill. As nomenclature goes, the category "brandy" covers, of course brandy, and also Pisco, Cognac, and other aged or unaged high proof spirits made from grapes. Pierre Ferrand 1840 Cognac and Macchu Pisco remain staples at my bar for their quality, versatility, and cocktailing heritage.

Cordials: This term largely covers the remaining array of high proof spirits. While brandy enjoys its own category, pretty well all the remaining fruit or spice spirits are considered cordials. Some cream spirits get shelved alongside these but they have little place in serious cocktailing.

More importantly, you will also find amaro spirits or "amari" stocked in the cordials section of your spirits shop. Italy reigns as the hallowed and largest producer of these intensely herbal and bitter spirits. Red aperitif amari like Campari and Cappelletti spark the appetite, while deep, dark digestifs like Fernet Branca help your tummy digest. Most bartenders hold both types of amari very close to their hearts for cocktails and toasting neat.

My home bar bursts with amari and other cordials. Knowing a sane person would not go to such lengths, here are some suggested staples that span many classic cocktails:

- Luxardo Maraschino
- Pierre Ferrand Dry Orange Curacao
- Cointreau or a sweet orange equivalent
- Allspice or Pimento Dram
- A reputable apple brandy or applejack
- Averna or a similar amaro
- Campari
- Chartreuse (green)

Whew. I hope this exhaustive list discourages no one from heading to your local spirits agency or peeling that sticker off the new credit card. Because we're not quite done.

Vermouth, aromatized wine, and fortified wine: These lower proof spirits shake hands very well with high proof spirits. They "modify" or compliment and mellow out stronger high proof spirits using lower proof flavors. Hence bartenders commonly call these spirits "modifiers."

Like amari, Italy makes most of the hallowed brands of vermouth and other aromatized wines, though respected examples also come from France, Spain, and other countries (occasionally the U.S. and Canada). Simply put, vermouth and other aromatized wines are hearty red or white wines around 17–20% ABV with highly-secretive blends of herbs.

Dry and red vermouth like Carpano should remain at hand in any worthwhile home bar. Good vermouths like these taste wonderful on their own, not just in cocktails. Bypass the serviceable grocery store brands like Stock or Martini & Rossi. Far superior brands and varieties await at most liquor agencies. Dry and red vermouth are musts, while sweeter bianco is more optional. Beyond vermouth, a dazzling array of aromatized wine awaits — Americano, Chinato, Quinaquina — accented with herbal flavors like gentian and quinine. Classic producers like Cocchi and Lillet should share the shelf with Carpano at any shop worth visiting. Keep these or any other aromatized wine chilled to prevent oxidation throughout their shelf life. Nothing turns me into more of an uppity asshole than being at a bar with dusty, unchilled vermouth bottles in plain sight.

Fortified wines like port, sherry, and madeira also grant you creative license. Producers "fortify" or strengthen these with a small portion of brandy. Sherry gave us classic cocktails like the Bamboo and the Sherry Cobbler. Meanwhile port or madeira afford you some fun creative alternatives to traditional cocktail components like vermouth.

Bitters

Imagine bitters as more concentrated amari. Bitters extract intense blends of herbs and other botanicals into a high proof spirit base. Only a few dashes or drops bind together all the spirits and other elements in a cocktail. I liken them to "the dude's rug" because they really tie the room together.

Any bar worth its salt features a classic aromatic bitter like Angostura, and probably orange bitters. The current explosion of craft bitters, however, spans into exotic flavors like tobacco, celery, rhubarb, and nut varieties. You can also make bitters at home using cheap vodka. Hey, look at that — a useful application for vodka!

Bitters come in two types of bottles. Some have built-in spouts or flow restrictors that let you shake dashes of bitters from the bottle. Others have eyedroppers that you use to draw out the bitters then squeeze out each dash. A "dash" is actually two shakes from a flow-restrictor bottle or 2–3 drops from an eyedropper. Remember this when recipes call for a certain number of "dashes."

That briefly sums up the spirit universe for an aspiring home mixologist. Be warned that I'll often call out for more peculiar spirits in the recipe chapters to come. Read onward for a summary of non-alcoholic cocktail elements and how these balance out the combined drink's ultimate flavor.

Chapter 2: The Bedfellows of Booze

Everything in the prior chapter comprises only a single flavor element in cocktails: spirit. And honestly, if you're only going to make "spirit-forward," full-on booze-and-bitters drinks then, well, you could skirt by on the stuff covered before this paragraph.

In truth, four more flavor elements come into play: sweet, "sour" or acidity, bitter, and "umami" or savory. Bitters and amari typically provide your bitter aspect — lending any kind of herbal influence you want in the mix. But you often need other means to express sweet, sour, or umami, even if using spirits that have these taste sensations.

Sweet = Syrups:

"Creme" or sweet spirits like creme de violette can fill the sweet part of the equation. But more often than not, cocktails need some form of sugar syrup. "Simple" or a 50/50 mix of sugar is most common. "Rich" simple uses less water and obviously ups the sweetness using less ounces of syrup.

Cocktail companies do make simple syrup. But making your own will save significant money. Just boil equal parts water and sugar until the sugar dissolves. Refrigerating the solution preserves it for quite a long time. Bear in mind that you can use any type of sugar: raw cane, demerara, brown, turbinado. Avoid refined sugar and spend a few more cents on good stuff.

With just one or two more steps, you can also home-make grenadine — a pomegranate syrup found in many classic cocktails. Proper grenadine in no way resembles Rose's grenadine, thank goodness. Good grenadine simply combines 100% pomegranate juice with an equal portion of simple syrup. A capful of rose water really makes this mix pop.

Practically any other syrup works in cocktails too: maple, honey, agave, or molasses. Seasonal drinks often call for these. Store-bought examples will work, but must be diluted with an equal portion of hot water. Undiluted syrups not only pour too slowly, but will prove too difficult to dilute when you mix a drink.

Beyond these easy, basic syrups, cocktails sometimes call for more exotic sweeteners like fruit, nut, or spice syrups — you'll find these more labor intensive. As long as I find a reputable and affordable source, I have no reservations leaving the heavy lifting to craft syrup producers. But the more personal touches you put on cocktails will raise your bragging rights. Plentiful recipes exist online. In most cases you end up boiling fruits, nuts, or spices with simple syrup.

Just about any imaginable fruit takes the form of a syrup in the world of cocktails. Passion fruit syrup, for example, commonly sweetens classic tiki cocktails. Tiki drinks and other modern classics often call for orgeat (an almond syrup) and falernum (a close relative enhanced with cloves or other spices).

23

Sour/Acidity = Fruits and Juices:

Visit the shot-and-beer bars with the most remote interest in making a cocktail and you will still find lemon, lime, and orange — either as fruits or juice or both. This tells us that the pairing of juice and spirits comes too naturally to overlook. They also help to balance the sweetness of syrups and sweeter spirits.

Though lemon and lime bite most sharply, they pair perfectly with all spirits in the spectrum and so many other cocktail components. Orange and grapefruit follow as very close seconds. More unusual forms of citrus like blood orange, tangerine, yuzu, and sudachi are ramping up their presence as the cocktail culture continues to gain creative momentum.

Non-citrus fruit juices like berry, apple, pear, and pomegranate obviously give you different flavors and lesser volumes of acidity. The best creative resource for pairing these flavors with spirits or other drink components is The Flavor Bible by Karen Page. Although this book is aimed at chefs, it's also an invaluable tool for mixologists creating drinks.

Always use the freshest juice possible. Squeeze citrus right from the fruit for the best flavor. Fresh citrus also gives you ready garnishes with fresh citrus peel oils. Garnish gives you aromatics, not just better eye candy on your drink. If you must use bottled juice, seek out 100% non-concentrate juice and use it before the freshness date ends. Juices from concentrates practically double the acid harshness of their natural equivalents.

Be adventurous and inspired when you find unusual juices at the grocer, too. Let the juice guide your creative process after you find it. After I discovered organic elderberry juice at the store, the resulting gin cocktail would end up being one of the best and most popular drinks I offered throughout a menu season.

Umami/Savory:

"Umami" describes flavors outside the sweet, bitter, and sour spectrum covered above. Imagine all the vegetal tastes like celery or squash that are less common but surely have a place in cocktails. Shrub cocktails that use a small portion of vinegar would also fall into the savory realm. Vegetables like cilantro, carrot, and tomato likewise give you savory flavors that can work wonderfully in cocktails.

Before I blather on endlessly about the cornucopia of flavors you can find at Whole Foods alone, we'd best get on with bar tools. You'll have enough of a shopping list once you get to the recipes.

Good bar tools needn't be costly, but don't buy the cheapest you can find. If this book saves you a wasted trip to a crummy restaurant supply store, it's at least accomplished something.

Let's kick off with measuring tools: jiggers. Good jiggers give you multiple measuring lines in a single piece. Cheap jiggers, on the other hand, usually only give you two measurements: 1 oz and ½ oz. The "Leopold" hourglass design and the tall, conical Japanese style (shown opposite page) let you accurately measure out ¼, ½, ¾, 1, 1½, and 2 oz. Their ergonomic shape makes them easy to pour by holding them by the center.

Like jiggers, a good shaker is equally important. You will almost always need to shake cocktails that include juices, creams, eggs, or egg whites with ice in order to fully blend them with spirits. The shaking also provides essential dilution that dials back the drink's intensity. And nothing is more irritating than shakers that leak when you shake.

The iconic style of shaker that most people visualize is the "cobbler" shaker you'd see on *Mad Men*. Ironically, this three-piece design leask when you shake but refuses to come apart when you're done shaking. I strongly recommend the "Boston" shaker shown on the opposite page. This simple two-piece design forms a better seal for shaking.

Boston shakers typically have an 18 oz top tin and a 28 oz bottom tin. Some sets use a pint-sized shaking glass instead of a smaller tin. These are heavier, don't seal as well, and are breakable. Seek out the "tin-on-tin" version if you want what most pro bartenders prefer.

A Boston shaker requires an accompanying "Hawthorne" strainer. After shaking, this tool holds back the ice as you pour out your shaken beverage. A coiled spring seats the strainer in the shaker while the perforated plate holds back the ice. The example shown to the left has a tight, strong coil that gives better results. Lower cost Hawthorne strainers wear out with continued use, and the coil often bends and even falls out of the strainer. This lets more ice chips seep through the strainer.

Method:
- When preparing shaken cocktails, measure and add your non-spirit into the larger shaker tin first. It hurts less to discard mismeasured ingredients before your more expensive spirit ingredients are added. After all liquids are measured in, fill the large tin about 2/3 full with ice. Pouring these over ice will start dilution before you even begin shaking.
- Place the smaller tin into the larger tin at an angle, as shown. Use one hand to smack or pound the small tin into the large tin, forming a seal. Shake the tins back and forth with some upward and downward movement for 20–30 seconds (more dense ice cubes require longer shaking). Smack the side of the larger tin to break the seal.
- Hold the Hawthorne strainer on top of the larger tin and pour the mix into your glass. If making a drink on the rocks, fresh ice in the glass will melt more slowly.

Cocktails that don't need shaking are stirred instead. Stirring blends and chills cocktails made with only spirits and bitters. This gentler method also adds about 25% dilution to the finished drink. Shaking "spirit forward" mixtures dilutes the drink too rapidly. If you see a bartender shake a Manhattan, remember the Supreme Court has roundly rejected prior restraint.

You will, however, sometimes shake drinks containing egg white. This adds a foamy texture to the drink. Egg white blends in very reluctantly and requires longer, more vigorous shaking.

Plan to "dry shake" without ice first, then add ice and shake again. This blends in the egg white without over-diluting.

Cocktail bartenders traditionally stir spirits in mixing glasses like the one shown shown on the opposite page. The heavy base lets you stir the mixture without holding the glass in place. Varying sizes and designs are available. A standard 16 oz glass holds a single cocktail and ice. A 24 oz mixing glass holds two to three portions.

Most bartenders use a traditional "julep" strainer to hold back used ice in a mixing glass. This spoon-style strainer works like a Hawthorne strainer without a coiled spring.

A mixing glass is not essential but it does make stirs easier. A 16 oz shaker pint glass serves the basic need but requires you to hold the glass while stirring. Likewise, a Hawthorne strainer can actually serve the same purpose as a julep strainer when using a 16 oz mixing glass or shaker pint. So again you have the option to side-step one additional tool. But why skip the chance to impress your friends with a fancy bit of kit?

You should, however, find a suitable bar spoon to stir your drinks regardless of the stirring vessel. The photo on the opposite page shows a very good bar spoon that is not expensive. As you see, this design has a very thin stem with a very tight spiral shape. This design makes it easier to stir a cocktail using your wrist and fingertips without breaking up the ice and over-diluting the mixture. Do not settle for the $3 bar spoon with the red plastic tip.

Method:
- Measure and add your ingredients into the mixing glass. After all ingredients are in the glass, fill it about 2/3 full of ice so that the ice level exceeds the liquid level.
- Hold the spoon between your fingers and rest the back surface of the spoon against the inner wall of the mixing glass. Using your wrist and fingertips, rotate the spoon so that the spoon remains against the inside wall of the glass. As you stir, the ice should spin as a single mass. Dense ice requires up to 50 stirs, while rapidly melting ice only needs 25–30.
- After the ice layer melts down and drops, strain the mixture into your drinking vessel.

It's important to perfect your stirring method as described above. I've opened bars and painstakingly trained people in this method, only to see them bashing a bar spoon wantonly through the ice in a mixing glass like they're stirring Kool-Aid. Not only will this make you look like a blundering novice, but your drinks will end up like spirit-flavored water. Good stirring method will actually hypnotize observers with delight, especially when you learn to stir two different drinks at the same time.

Mixing glasses and bar spoons can get ornate and more expensive. You just need to decide how posh you want to get with your bar tools. Among the plethora of other tools you can get, only a muddler is really essential. You use this to "muddle" or press flavor and aroma oils from plants like citrus peel or mint in certain cocktail mixtures. Mojitos and Old Fashioneds are good examples of classic muddled cocktails.

Muddlers are made from wood, metal, or dense plastics. While all of these are suitable, wood is the longer-standing tradition. Should you choose a wooden muddler, select a bare wood design. Coatings like varnish will eventually chip off after continued use. You can also find bar spoons that have makeshift muddlers at the end of the stem.

Oooh! I almost forgot! You'll probably want a "Y" peeler too. This Y-shaped tool lets you easily peel skin from any citrus fruit for use in garnishing or muddling. A good brand like Oxo can be found in most home goods departments. The best brand I've used is Kuhn.

This concludes your ten-cent tour through basic bar tools. Don't worry, little hobbits. I'll get you back to the Shire in due course.

I'd be remiss if I didn't talk at least briefly about the ice you use to chill your drinks and keep them cold, much less the vessels that hold them. Those that aren't professionals or at least strong enthusiasts might ask, "Why is he actually making me read about frozen water? Ice is just … ice." Well … not exactly.

When I was still a novice, industry friends would bring coolers of ice from their bar to our house for me to use in their cocktails. I won't get into the hard-knocks stirring training that ensued. I quickly discovered that good ice machines produced superior ice that didn't melt as quickly. But my initial reaction was "really?"

I'm willing to bet you too have sipped on drinks that diluted rapidly, even at bars with good drink programs. I'd also wager that these bars invested heavily in everything else and then settled for a less reputable ice machine. I've been there. I've recommended good ice machines to launch new bars and regrettably been talked out of them. Not only did my cocktails suffer, but I had to magically fill the barren space in everyone's glass that resulted from hollow ice cubes. If you're reading this, you know who you are.

Home bartenders don't lose sleep over these things. But it still makes sense to consider quality ice. It's ok to shake and stir with porous ice as long as you consider that it melts more quickly, and adjust your shakes or stirs accordingly. The same ice will, however, also melt quickly when you use it to keep your finished cocktails cold in a glass.

I have the luxury of living in an area where producers make good, dense ice in bulk freezer bags. This makes bartending at home for larger groups much easier. Additionally, silicone rubber ice cube trays help sustain a ready supply of cubes in a variety of sizes. These include the 1-inch cubes to use for shaking and stirring, and the 2-inch cubes and spheres that keep a good Negroni cold in the glass. The latter are called "large format" ice.

Silicone ice cube trays might prove easiest to find online. Most stores don't stock them, and even major cities are lucky to have stores that specialize in cocktail tools. You might also consider online sources to obtain two more ice tools: a Lewis bag and a "schmallet" or wooden hammer. They let you cheaply and easily create crushed ice if your refrigerator does not have a versatile, built-in ice machine.

Tiki cocktails commonly call for crushed ice. These cocktails often contain 6–10 ingredients, most of which are rums or other spirits. It makes sense to cool these with quicker-melting crushed ice simply because of the potent spirits and flavors. When these or any other cocktail calls for crushed ice, put your cubes in the Lewis bag and break them up with the schmallet.

Lastly you'll want to keep a few traditional styles of drink vessels around: Collins, rocks and coupe glasses. Collins glasses hold drinks that are poured over 1-inch ice cubes. Tall, refreshing spring and summer drinks often call for these. Shorter, shallower rocks glasses can instead hold larger 2-inch cubes or spheres. These will keep strong, spirit-focused concoctions cold for a longer time without melting as quickly.

The recipes in this book do call for some other more exotic vessels, but you can run a fully functioning home bar with the core styles described above. And you'd be amazed at the range of vintage and exotic glassware you can find at a thrift store.

Conversely, use coupes to serve chilled cocktails "up" or without ice. Hold these vessels by the stem so that your hand does not in turn warm up the cocktail. Smaller traditional coupes only hold about 4 oz of liquid and spill quite easily, much like martini glasses which I've always found to be a flawed design. Larger 6–8 oz coupes leave you room for slightly larger cocktails with less danger of spills.

You will commonly see bartenders chill a coupe glass with ice and sometimes water or soda water while mixing the cocktail. After discarding the cooling ice, this theoretically keeps the cocktail cold a little bit longer while you drink it.

Okay. Now go buy all your drink vessels and tools. Don't worry, I can wait.

Now that you have everything you need, we'll end this fairly long-winded chapter with some classic cocktail recipes. These don't just help you learn technique; they also show you how to nip and tuck recipes to your liking.

I've left wiggle room in the following builds, very much on purpose. These give you the option of stronger spirit presence, and more or less sweetness or acidity. Tweak each recipe to your preferences or those of your guests. Bear in mind you will begin with about 3 ounces liquids when building, then yield about 4 ounces total after shaking or stirring.

Practice Round 1: The Classic Martini

I learned painful lessons about Martinis when starting professional bartending. In the strictest definition, gin, dry vermouth, and sometimes light bitters comprise a martini. After learning that Martinis require you to interrogate a guest, you may ultimately discover that they want 3 ounces of chilled vodka. These people should face criminal charges, but you can't stifle freedom of choice, no matter how fucking stupid those choices might be.

Nor do Martinis include the vulgar diabetic concoctions of chocolate, vanilla, and other absurdities. If your friends ask you for these, you should really question whether you remain friends. Don't stock your bar with the filth necessary to make these war-crime level atrocities. Then you won't have to even worry about making them.

The first question is the base spirit. If it's vodka, convince them to use gin. I don't condone threats of violence, but nor do I condemn them. Then figure out what brand of GIN should be used. I'm not apologizing. Just drink gin, god damn it.

Then decide how dry you or your guest wants this drink. More vermouth renders a sweeter drink. "Bone dry" means you simply rinse the glass with a swish of vermouth. Vermouth lovers like myself sometimes ask for the 50/50 Martini, calling for equal parts gin and vermouth. If they say no vermouth, you reply "that's not a martini," possibly concluding the sentence with "idiot." I would choose the latter option.

Orange bitters really tie these elements together with a nice floral bow. But so many light and fitting bitters are available now: Elderflower, lavender, plum. You really can go nuts. And if your guest insists on vodka, sneak these in without asking. They might be astounded to actually taste something.

If you have not yet burned this book out of frustration with my smugness, the martini build is as follows:

- 1.5 to 3 oz gin (1.5 for a 50/50, or up to 3 oz for the "bone-dry" version)
- ¼ to 1.5 oz vermouth (balance the remainder with the gin to come up with 3 oz)
- 1–2 dashes orange or other floral bitters of your choice (optional)

Chill a coupe glass with ice. Add your spirit(s) to the mixing glass and stir. Discard the ice from the coupe. If going for bone-dry, swish the vermouth around in the glass and discard. Strain the stirred mix into the coupe.

A lemon peel twist accents this simple classic very nicely. "Express" the peel or twist it over the drink surface to get the lemon oil aromatics. Then coil up the peel and pierce with a cocktail skewer before resting it on the edge of the glass. Personally I can't stand olive garnishes, much less mold-infested blue cheese olives. And don't get me started on the whole "dirty" thing. If you need salty olive juice to get a martini down your craw, then don't drink martinis.

And now, on to another underrated and misunderstood classic.

Practice Round 2: The Margarita

Dreadful Margarita failures can blame the cheap sour mix with which they are commonly made. If you instead use fresh lime juice and good simple syrup, guests often rave that they've just tasted the best Margarita (even if you're stuck using an inexpensive mixto). Reliance on sour mix is a true disservice to a simple and exquisite cocktail, even at authentic Mexican restaurants.

Follow this simple recipe instead. About half the time the drinker will prefer a salt rim on the glass, presumably to counter the citrus acidity of the drink. You can do this whether you serve it "up" or on the rocks.

- 1.5–2 oz aged or unaged 100% agave tequila
- ¾–1 oz orange cordial spirit (Patron Citronge or Agavero work nicely; avoid cheap triple sec)
- ¾–1 oz fresh-squeezed lime juice
- ½ oz simple syrup (optional, but essential in my mind to balance acidity)

Shake everything with ice. If a salt rim is preferred, cut the pulp of a lime wedge and coat the edge of the glass with citrus juice, then dip the glass in a plate of good coarse sea salt. Strain the mixture into the glass. Rest the lime wedge on the edge of the glass as a garnish.

Practice Round 3: The Classic Daiquiri

The frozen, sickly-sweet drive-thru daiquiris that New Orleans made famous have poisoned the cocktail world; not simply by virtue of their horrid taste, but also by convincing the world that these are the world's only expression of the daiquiri. Mind you that good and proper frozen cocktails are out there — you just have to look pretty hard.

The classic daiquiri is a work of simple genius: rum, lime, and simple syrup, served up. Period. A good friend in the industry calls this the perfect cocktail and I'm inclined to agree. It works with any style of rum and really lets you experience this broad spirit realm in the form of a cocktail. Many pro bartenders even greet their guests and industry pals with mini-daiquiris, lovingly known as "snack-quiris."

Play with the daiquiri recipe below to find your sweet spot (or less sweet spot, really). You can up the spirit portion or dial it back, and balance out the remaining syrup and lime components to suit your preference for sweet or sour. In the end you'll be shaking 3 total ounces of liquid:

- 1.5 to 2 oz rum
- ½ to 1 oz fresh lime juice
- ½ to 1 oz simple syrup (demerara or turbinado add character but raw sugar is fine)

Shake everything with ice and strain the mix into a chilled coupe glass. Lay a thin lime wheel on the drink surface to garnish.

Practice Round 4: The Manhattan

I'm not even going to hint at the origin of the name. That's a fucking rabbit hole for another day. Suffice it to say it's another three-ingredient classic for good reason.

You don't really see many barkeeps messing with the proportions in a Manhattan, but you can switch up the base spirit, the modifier, and the bitters. If you prefer drier and spicier over sweet, switch the base bourbon to rye. If you want more sweet above herbal notes, use sherry or madeira instead of vermouth. And don't feel limited to classic aromatic bitters; play with cinnamon, coffee, or cocoa bitters. I guarantee every iteration will work.

Here's your standard issue build:

- 2 oz bourbon or rye
- 1 oz aromatized or fortified wine
- 2 dashes bitters

Stir it up and strain it into a chilled cocktail glass, then garnish with a skewered, brandied cocktail cherry. Thank you for forging your way through Chapter 2. If you want to get funky, read onward.

Chapter 3: Under the Influence

All the barkeeps I know cut their teeth on time-tested cocktails. Decades have proven that drinks like Old Fashioneds, Martinis, and sours can survive not just at high-end cocktail bars, but also at most musty neighborhood watering holes. The forebears of cocktailing gave us such well-balanced, simple staples that every bartender really can't avoid committing them to memory; guests order them so often the builds just become muscle memory.

Sure, OG cocktailing ancestors like Jerry Thomas and Harry Craddock literally created a genre using the early staple ingredients at their disposal. Some unknown bar soldiers also birthed cocktails of legend. No one can conclusively say who created the Manhattan or Margarita. Yet these creations enjoy eternal life at bars across the globe.

So you might ask, why mess with a good thing?

Mixologists still in their infancy do well to create what's called "drinks of influence." Also called "riffs," these are simply twists on time-tested classic recipes. After serving up the, frankly, now unavoidable vintage drinks like Manhattans day after day, you start to think "how can I tweak this for fun." You start flipping sherry in place of the vermouth. You change the bitters or even blend two bitters. Maybe even add a new spirit to the mix. And there you have your first drink of influence.

This chapter gives you some of the riffs on classics I've noodled together over the years. I hope these recipes give you some direction creating your own. More often than not, you'll find that they work out well.

Let's Call It a Tai

In my mind, I'd only call myself a "professional" of about five years. And only within the past year could I answer this question with any conviction:

"What is your favorite cocktail to drink/make?"

It's the 1944 Mai Tai, no question. No cocktail has ever offered the balance and versatility of this recipe. Arguments still wage over its invention, whether by "Trader Vic" Bergeron or "Don the Beachcomber," decades ago during the golden age of tiki cocktails that they spearheaded. While evidence suggests Don as the true grandfather of tiki, Vic made the Mai Tai his signature drink. Hence, it's commonly called the "Trader Vic Mai Tai."

Many horrific interpretations also adopted the name Mai Tai, often taking the form of overly sweet, pink to red, pint-sized atrocities served in Chinese restaurants. Only the 1944/Trader Vic version boasts any merit. All versions include rum, but only the heritage recipe holds any merit and balances flavors effectively.

What I discovered over about 10 years pursuing tiki is that the proper Mai Tai is so well-balanced and versatile that you can replace the base spirit with near impunity. Gin, tequila, and rye versions all work a treat. The rest of the build stays the same, easy peasy. I only regret that committing these simple variations to print will lessen what little perceived genius I have garnered across the bar.

Let's start with the modifying ingredients:

- ¾ oz fresh lime juice
- ¼ oz simple syrup
- ¼ oz orgeat
- ½ oz dry orange curacao

For the classic rum version, add: 1 oz light rum and 1 oz dark (Jamaican preferred)
For the gin version, add: 1 oz London dry gin and 1 oz Old Tom gin
For the rye version, add 2 oz rye, and ¼ oz blackstrap rum for added zing

Shake it all up with ice and strain over fresh ice in a rocks glass. Garnish with fresh mint sprig.

Always in Fashion

Working at any cocktail bar, no matter how high end or off-center it may be, you can expect to make multiple Old Fashioneds on any given night. Bourbon mania has seen to that. It's well within the comfort zone of the cocktail-phobic, since it's about as close to a bourbon rocks as you can get.

Despite its simplicity, the Old Fashioned retains timeless status because the flavors it marries are a heavenly match. To exercise a little creativity and expand the horizons of guests that order multiple OFs, I developed the riff below. It highlights my fondness for wheated bourbons and ups the spice factor on your standard OF.

Fairytale of Bourbon County

- 2 oz wheated bourbon such as Maker's Mark (100% wheat whiskey works well too)
- ½ oz cinnamon clove syrup
- ¼ oz Barrows Intense Ginger
- 2 dashes Bittercube Vanilla Cherry Bark Bitters
- Orange peel

Add syrup, bitters, and a strip of orange peel into the mixing glass and muddle the peel with the liquids. Add the spirits and fill the glass with ice above the liquid level. Stir until adequately diluted. Strain mixture over a large format ice cube. Extract the peel from the mixing glass and lay it on the ice cube.

Brooklyn Revisited

Less people know the Brooklyn cocktail, but I find it equal in merit to the Old Fashioned. It balances rye, dry vermouth, Luxardo Maraschino cordial, and Picon orange cordial perfectly. It felt a little dirty to trifle with it. But imitation is a form of flattery, after all. This version takes a slightly sweeter tack using bianco vermouth, and uses Bonal to bring out the herbal notes.

I guess the spin below is technically a "New Brooklyn," but I felt compelled to name it after one of Cleveland's beloved boroughs.

The Old Brooklyn

- 2 oz Michter's Rye
- ¾ oz Carpano Bianco Vermouth
- ¼ oz Luxardo
- ¼ oz Bonal

Measure all spirits into the mixing glass and top with ice above the liquid level. Stir until mixture is adequately diluted. Strain into a chilled cocktail glass.

From the Bar at the Iceberg Lounge

I don't just geek out about cocktails. I also nerd out on comic books. You're actually going to see a number of cocktails that in some way affirm my adoration for graphic novelty. Good spirits help me nod off into dreamland as much as anyone. But honestly, I need a good comic book to usher me to sleep every night.

The cocktail below simultaneously pays tribute to a classic cocktail and a classic pulp villain: the Sherry Cobbler and the Penguin, respectively. Good sherry, in my opinion, does not share enough of the spotlight with other modifiers like vermouth. And let's face it — the Penguin was a short, obese man that fought with an umbrella. This amped-up version of the Cobbler gives them the props they deserve.

The Oswald Cobblerpot

- 1 oz Nolet's Silver Gin
- ¾ oz Byrrh
- ¾ oz lemon juice
- ½ oz gomme syrup
- 4 dashes Bittermens Burlesque bitters
- ½ oz Carcavelos
- Blueberries or berry mix for muddling
- Swedish fish garnish (optional)

Muddle berries, syrup, and lemon juice in the large shaker tin. Add all remaining liquids except sherry. Shake with ice. Strain into rocks glass. Add crushed ice to a slight mound above the drink surface. Slowly pour the sherry over the ice, then dash the bitters over the ice. Garnish with additional berries and Swedish fish candy (if available).

Learn to Fly

The next few drinks in this section bow to the gods of tiki. If you don't like tiki, jump to Chapter 4. But if this is the case, I'm not sure we can stay friends.

Working at a tiki bar, you often need to probe a guest's flavor preferences fairly deeply. With so many ingredients in the mix, a single one of these can derail someone's fondness for a pretty expensive beverage. Six drops of Pernod will force anyone who hates licorice to push a drink back to you.

But for the adventurous, I always steer patrons towards the Jet Pilot. It ticks all of the check boxes I love about tiki: strong and complex rum, bitters and spices, lime and grapefruit. To make this drink more approachable, I ended up creating a mildly sweeter and bubbly version of it. The main hitch will be finding grapefruit and lime sodas, but it's well worth the effort.

Another fun option is pebble ice for the drink vessel. Large bags can be purchased at any Sonic location for about $2.50.

Tropical Turbulence

- 1 oz Appleton Estate Rum
- ¾ oz Bounty Gold Rum
- ¾ oz Hamilton 151
- 1 dash Angostura Aromatic Bitters
- 6 drops Pernod
- ½ oz cinnamon syrup
- ½ oz falernum cordial (Velvet or Maggie's Farm)
- Lime and grapefruit sodas

Shake all but bitters, Pernod, and sodas with ice. Strain over crushed or pebble ice in a tall Collins glass. Fill the balance of the glass with even amounts of both sodas. Drip Pernod and bitters on the ice surface. Garnish with a lime wedge.

Devilish Bastard

This one's more of a mash-up than drink of influence, perhaps. It's an unholy wedding between the Suffering Bastard and the El Diablo. Traditionally both cocktails share ginger beer and lime. This version borrows tequila and blackcurrant spirit from the El Diablo, and the brandy and bitters from the Suffering Bastard. The little tweaks on both recipes make for a very enjoyable cocktail.

Suffering Diablo

- 1 oz Altos Anejo Tequila
- ½ oz falernum cordial (Maggie's Farm or Bitter Truth)
- ½ oz plum brandy
- ½ oz fresh lime juice
- ¼ oz Ferrand crème de cassis
- ¼ oz agave syrup
- Ginger beer
- Bittermens Mole Bitters

Shake all but ginger beer and bitters. Strain over ice in a tall Collins glass. Fill the balance with ginger beer and drizzle a layer of bitters on top. Garnish with a lemon wheel.

Heavier Artillery

The cocktail dorks among us know that the French 75 takes its name from a 75mm artillery shell. It's a bubbly gin classic that's remained popular since 1927. In the spirit of more boastful ordnance, I took it upon myself to tiki-fy the 75 using French-owned Plantation rums. My version gets a little extra fortification from madeira.

Yes, that pun works on two levels.

Polynesian 75

    1 oz Plantation 3 Star Rum

    1 oz Plantation Stiggins' Fancy Pineapple Rum

    ½ oz madeira

    ½ oz fresh lemon juice

    ½ oz simple syrup

    Prosecco (La Marca or Mionetto)

Shake all ingredients except prosecco with ice. Strain mixture into a champagne flute. Top with prosecco, to taste. Garnish with a lemon peel.

Sideways Sidecar

The Sidecar cocktail has an interesting heritage. First introduced in print in 1922, it's the brainchild of a London bartender, built upon two classic French spirits: Cointreau and cognac. And unless you go to a serious cocktail bar that embraces heritage cocktails, you don't often see them.

Much like my 75 spin above, my sidecar riff again calls for great spirits from the parent company of Plantation, Pierre Ferrand. I make no qualms that I adore their whole portfolio. The sidecar interpretation below also employs craft lemon soda to express the citrus component, and get some extra zing from aromatic orange accents.

The recipe below takes its name from a bygone French motorcycle manufacturer. This is also an example of cocktails you can "build in the glass" or mix directly in the drink vessel.

Motobecane

    ½ oz Pierre Ferrand Dry Orange Curacao

    1.5 oz Pierre Ferrand 1840 Cognac

    Craft lemon soda (use Fever Tree Bitter Lemon for a sharper, drier effect)

    2 drops orange blossom water

    Add ice into a tall Collins glass. Pour in spirits and soda, then drip orange blossom water on the surface. Garnish with an orange wedge.

Chapter 4: Highballs, Elevated to Collins*

Another minor hurdle I found bartending was explaining the term "highball" to patrons. The term broadly describes any cocktail that simply combines spirit with a soda. It covers your gin & tonic, rum & Coke, whiskey & ginger, and lest we forget the flavor bonanza of vodka & soda. Yeah, kiss my ass. You try making ten at a time for a bunch of selfie poseurs and spray tan models, then we can talk.

One of the first bars at which I took the reins of the drink program was a specialty highball bar. It sprung from Old City Soda, Cleveland's first true bespoke soda company. The sodas were so expertly crafted, in fact, it made a bartender's job way too easy. Just mix a spirit with the soda and you already have a delectable adult beverage.

So it made perfect sense to launch a companion highball bar called Old City Libations in Cleveland's happening Gordon Square neighborhood. From an execution standpoint, it was just too easy to pair and serve spirits with the house sodas. I took it upon myself to make my job harder, and make cocktails that raised more eyebrows. Which basically meant elevating the menu options to Collins and fizzes, alongside the easier highballs.

Blending shaken cocktails with some form of soda is nothing new. Take the Tom Collins, which combines the effervescence of club soda with shaken gin, lemon, and simple syrup. It just takes a two-ingredient highball up a couple notches, but enough notches to make it a timeless classic. The recipes that follow carry on this spirit.

Several of the recipes in this chapter call for fairly unusual craft sodas. You don't necessarily need to seek out bottled versions from soda companies. Instead, you can easily find a craft syrup with the correct flavor, then blend this with club soda. The same option applies with craft tonic syrups, which let you easily make tonics in a variety of flavors.

It begs the obvious, but the soda component is always added after all non-carbonated, shaken ingredients are in the drinking glass. You'd be baffled by how many people I know that learned not to shake carbonated liquids the hard way.

(*And Phil, if you're reading this, you suck. Though your daughter is quite fetching.)

That Voodoo that I Do

I'm not sure how my colleagues begin creating their drinks. Personally I find that one of two things happen. One: A really clever drink name hits me and I let that inspire the recipe. Two: Ideas on flavor combinations unfold into a cocktail, which then inspires how I name the drink. The cocktail below resulted from the latter.

So you may be asking, "Did he name this after that weird 1988 Wes Craven movie?" Well, yes. And I have no idea why. Maybe I was drunk. It sounds cool though, doesn't it? I suspect it relates to the dual apple ingredients. And there was some book that said serpents like apples. The name escapes me.

On a less mysterious note, the cocktail below resulted from an unexpected find at the grocery store. Unless you're shopping at a really crummy grocer, you can stumble across ingredients that drive you to create a drink. This one can thank the happy accident of finding Fuji apple soda.

Serpent and the Rainbow

- 1 oz Calvados
- 1 oz Redemption Bourbon
- 2 oz Dry Brand Fuji Apple Soda
- ½ oz Lillet Rouge
- ¼ oz agave syrup
- ½ oz fresh lemon juice

Shake all but soda and Lillet with ice and pour mixture over fresh ice in a Collins glass. Add soda to near top. Sink Lillet Rouge to bottom. Garnish with a dried apple.

I'm Coming to Join You, Elizabeth

Being on the staff of a tiki bar or classic cocktail bar, you'd eventually make something with St. Elizabeth Allspice Dram, or a close relative like Bitter Truth or Hamilton Pimento Dram. Even just a quarter-ounce has a tremendous pimento spice impact on any cocktail. The recipe below attests to its honored place in Caribbean cocktails.

Elizabeth, My Dear

- ¾ oz fresh key lime juice
- ½ oz honey syrup
- ¼ oz St Elizabeth Allspice Dram
- ½ oz Cruzan Blackstrap Rum
- 1.5 oz Angostura White Oak Rum
- Grapefruit soda

Shake all but soda with ice, then strain mixture over fresh ice in a rocks glass. Top with soda, then garnish with mint and lime wheel.

I'd Just as Soon Stay Sick

When launching a new cocktail bar in 2018, I worked very hard on the opening seasonal menu. Twelve cocktails were road-tested and carefully named. Two days after taste testing, the GM insisted that all the bar's cocktails should bear a Cleveland-related name of some kind. If you live here, you can guess how difficult this could get after the first two years, much less on one already completed menu.

After about 30 minutes of arguing with the GM on the phone (and weaving a tapestry of profanities while on mute), I conceded and set about renaming all 12 cocktails. The CLE concept eventually garnered the bar a "best Cleveland-themed cocktails" award in one of our local periodicals. Nothing like media validation of a short-sighted idea to help exacerbate my anger.

When the time came for the 2nd seasonal menu, I decided that if I'm painted into this corner, I'm devoting the entire cocktail menu to Cleveland punk bands: Pere Ubu, The Dead Boys, The Electric Eels, the Pagans, and of course, The Cramps. First order of business was to develop a very luxurious cocktail honoring Lux Interior, the sadly departed Cramps frontman. I hope you'll find this a fitting memorial. You'll always stay sick in our memories, Lux.

Lux Interior

  1 egg white
  ¾ oz Lakewood Organic Tart Cherry Juice
  ½ oz spicy ginger syrup
  1.5 oz Aviation Gin
  ½ oz Maurin Le Puy Quina
  2 oz Q Club Soda
  2 candied ginger pieces, 1 brandied cherry

Crack the egg in half and carefully pass the yolk between shells, letting the egg white drop into the shaker. Add all remaining ingredients except club soda. Shake vigorously for 30–60 seconds. Add ice and shake for another 30 seconds. Strain the mixture into a Collins glass. Top with club soda until froth reaches the top. Skewer ginger, cherry, and second ginger piece onto skewer to use as garnish.

Bastard on Steroids

The drink below probably should go in the chapter on drinks of influence. But this chapter is pretty short. This is also another testimony to my love of Suffering Bastards. Perhaps because it originated as a hangover cure. It's tasty and simple, too.

I'd come to possess a crate of vintage Cleveland soda bottles, which convinced me to do a vintage-style bottled cocktail version. This was the result.

The Suffering Soda Jerk

- ½ oz lime juice
- 1 oz Opihr Gin
- 1 oz apple brandy
- Cock and Bull Cherry Lime Ginger Beer soda
- 3 dashes Bittermens 'Elemakule Tiki Bitters

Shake all but soda with ice. Strain the mixture over fresh ice in a tall Collins glass. Fill the balance with soda and dash bitters on the surface. Garnish with an orange wedge and mint sprig.

Splendor in the Glass

When Ancho Reyes finally came to Ohio, the first instinct was to spice up a tequila cocktail. So I did the opposite and made a peppery rum Collins. Not sure how I arrived at the name, as there is really nothing American about it.

American Splendor

- 1 oz Ancho Reyes
- 1.5 oz Mount Gay Black Barrel Rum
- ½ oz Luxardo Maraschino
- ½ oz agave syrup
- 1 oz lemon juice
- 1 oz Q Club Soda
- Lemon wheel and Amarena cherry flag garnish

Add all liquid ingredients into shaker with ice and shake mixture for 15 seconds. Strain mixture over fresh ice in a Collins glass. Top with club soda. Make a lemon wheel and cherry "flag" garnish and lay on drink surface.

Death Proof

Back when I was reimagining the aforementioned cocktail menu to compliment my fair city of residence, one drink on this menu became a curse. The drink bore the name of the infamous downtown highway curve littered with the bumpers from car accidents. The name didn't thrill me, but the cocktail became a bestseller.

So popular was it that it became a permanent fixture across every seasonal menu, much to the chagrin of the bar staff who hated shaking the egg whites. After about six seasonal menus, the cocktail was removed to make room for new drink creations. The ongoing requests for the cocktail ultimately forced it back on the menu the following season.

Below is a reimagining of the original cocktail that gives you a few options. The original cocktail got its sweetness from blueberries until they went out of season. The substituted blackberry approach worked equally well. This new version also calls for a Canadian pea flower infused gin, but any gin in the New Western category works well.

Dead Man's Curve Revisited

½ oz blackberry or blueberry syrup

½ oz Pickett's Medium Ginger Syrup

¾ oz lemon juice

1 egg white

1 oz Fever Tree Ginger Ale or Ginger Beer

2 oz Empress 1908 Indigo Gin

Skewered gummy bear garnish

Crack the egg in half and carefully pass the yolk between shells, letting the egg white drop into the shaker. Add all remaining ingredients except soda. Shake vigorously for 30–60 seconds. Add ice and shake for another 30 seconds. Strain the mixture into a Collins glass. Top with ginger soda until froth reaches the top. Skewer gummy bear through the heart and garnish.

Chapter 5: Under the Gin-fluence

Early in my mixology career, I tended bar at a specialty gin and cider bar. A barmy expat friend of mine from Herefordshire, England launched a local craft cider company, then later opened a bar to showcase these ciders. Being proudly English, he also decided to feature gin across 80% of the back bar.

Craft cider exploded in popularity and drew people to the bar from miles away. I found gin, on the other hand, a much harder sell, despite my own fervent adoration for the spirit. But this challenged me in the best way possible. It forced me to learn a wide spectrum of classic gin cocktails, create a compelling drink menu from scratch, and then develop some of my first signature drinks.

Perhaps this was providence. At the time I had one or two London Dry gins and maybe one Old Tom gin at home. Then, at work I had 60 gins to play with. Then 80. Then 90. Sure it's only one spirit category. But many greater geniuses in cocktailing started with a much smaller array of gins than I did.

This chapter pays tribute to those baby steps in mixology I was lucky enough to enjoy on someone else's dime … or ten pence, I suppose.

Smashed

Little known fact: creating cocktails can sometimes help you exorcise your nerdiest demons.

When "smash" cocktails became popular, it hit me that I had to come up with a "Hulk Smash." And it had to be green on top and purple on the bottom. The smash part was simple — just make sure it had green muddled fruit that stays in the finished drink. Thank goodness for Green Chartreuse and Bitter Truth Violet. I'd sooner die than make it with Midori. Equal thanks that Marvel Comics couldn't charge me with copyright infringement over a beverage.

The recipe worked a treat. Guests loved it and I made it my shift drink all season. It was providence that a Yellow Chartreuse and muddled lemon version would follow. I knew Cherry Heering would provide the red. So a friend that loved the DC Universe christened it the "Reverse Flash Smash." Seriously, DC, how many Flash characters do you need?

Both of these are "dirty pour" drinks. In other words, you pour the muddled items, mixed liquids, and ice directly into the glass, rather than strain over fresh ice. Both drinks also share the same build method — only the spirits and muddled materials differ.

Hulk Smash

- 1 oz Green Chartreuse
- 1 oz St. George Terroir Gin
- ½ oz Bitter Truth Violet (or other creme de violette)
- ½ oz honey syrup
- ½ lime cut into three wedges
- Mint leaves and stalk

Reverse Flash Smash

- 1 oz Yellow Chartreuse
- 1 oz St. George Terroir Gin
- ½ oz Cherry Heering or Luxardo Sangue Morlacco
- ½ oz honey syrup
- ½ lemon cut into three wedges

Muddle the citrus wedges (and some mint leaves for the Hulk version) in a shaker with the honey syrup. Add the Chartreuse and gin into the shaker with ice. Shake and then pour contents into rocks glass. Slowly pour the cordial spirit (violet or cherry) into the drink so that it sinks to the bottom of the glass.

For the Hulk Smash, add a lime wedge and mint sprig garnish. For the Flash version, add a skewered lemon wheel and brandied cherry garnish.

Whores of Babylon

The next sinful delight evolved from a cocktail originally invented for Dinner in the Dark, a Cleveland independent charity pop-up. Columbus distiller Middle West Spirits had just launched their 17-botanical Vim & Petal Gin, and I was eager to showcase this in a cocktail.

The original version leaned slightly sweet despite the compliment of lime. When it came time for a new seasonal menu at the bar, it merged with prosecco to make a drier, bubbly interpretation. The second iteration was named after a now-defunct indie music venue. Ironically, the space is now occupied by a wine bar and a cocktail bar.

Babylon-a-Go-Go

- 1.5 oz Vim & Petal Gin
- ½ oz Bonal
- ¾ oz lime
- ½ oz honey syrup
- ½ oz Mathilde Framboise cordial
- Prosecco float

Shake all but prosecco and strain into a flute. Top with bubbles. Garnish with a lime peel twist.

And Now for Something Completely Different

If you're reading this book word-for-word, you'll recall I once wandered past organic elderberry juice in a local grocer. In that moment, I knew it had to be in a cocktail. At that same time, I was struggling to come up with a cocktail that effectively included Grappa. Grappa comes from the discarded bits of grapes used for other spirits and can be a bit harsh. And I made it my mission to tame it.

If I need to explain the name, I suspect your address is written on a rock. Let's just say the name sold the cocktail the first time. Then it turned into a "come for the name, stay for the flavor" situation.

Your Mother was a Hamster

- 1.5 oz Watershed Guild Gin
- ½ oz simple syrup
- ½ oz Pear Nectar
- ½ oz Elderberry Juice
- ½ oz a Moscato a Nonino Grappa

Shake all ingredients with ice and strain over fresh ice in a Collins glass. Garnish with a fresh or dehydrated pear slice.

The Pickle Man

Yes, I can, in fact, recite the entire "Pickle Rick" episode of Rick and Morty. Can you? Can you create a pickle cocktail dedicated to Rick? No, I don't do magic, I do mixology. One takes brains, the other takes dark eye liner.

Farewell, Solenya

½ oz dill pickle brine (Use something good with actual dill weed in it, not Vlasic)

1.5 oz Death's Door Gin

½ oz lime juice

½ Tempus Fugit Kina l'Aero D'or Quinquina

2 dashes Bittermens Celery Shrub Bitters

Fever Tree Mediterranean Tonic

Shake all but tonic with ice. Strain over fresh ice in Collins. Top with tonic. Add pickle wedge garnish on skewer and dill stalk as garnish.

Styx Sucks, Let's Get that Straight

The company Haus Alpenz puts out a variety of truly amazing amaros and aromatized wines. It's probably one of my favorite spirit lines. Whenever they release something new, it's a cue that I have to get it into a cocktail, posthaste.

When Haus Alpenz introduced their Amaro Sfumato Rabarbaro (a rhubarb amaro), it was like seeing the bat signal in the night sky. And it had to have some other truly weird shit in it. The diabolical build below is what came out of the batcave.

Domo Arigato, Mr. Sfumato

½ oz Amaro Sfumato Rabarbaro

½ oz Ikkomon Shochu

1 oz Sanpellegrino Aranciata Rossa (Blood Orange)

1 oz Tanqueray 10 Gin

½ oz Patron Citronge Orange cordial

½ oz Strawberry puree

Rhubarb stalk and strawberry garnish

Add all but Sanpellegrino to a shaker and shake with ice. Strain into a tulip glass or snifter. Top with Sanpellegrino, to taste. Add rhubarb stalk and strawberry garnish.

Have Some Pride, You Savage

Of late, I've developed an appalling penchant for making cocktails using stuff from a jar that's meant to be used for gastronomical applications. One such example is chutney. Think about it — all those yummy savory and fruit flavors. It wasn't so much a challenge as it was making my job easier. Being that chutney is native to the British Isles, it made sense to base the drink on gin, hearkening back to the days that the sun actually didn't settle on the British Empire.

Pride, Prejudice & Headhunters

- 1.5 oz Oxley London Dry Gin
- Heaping bar spoon Mango Chutney
- 1 oz Madeira
- ½ oz fresh lime juice
- Mint garnish

Muddle chutney with lime in a large shaker tin. Add remaining ingredients and shake with ice. Strain mixture over a large format ice cube in a rocks glass. Garnish with a mint sprig.

Look what I've been Reduced to...

Visiting your friends' cocktail bars eventually becomes research to a degree. You enjoy their creations, and then maybe you borrow an idea or two. At one point, I noticed some uses of wine reductions.

I'll be honest. I've never been a wine guy. I like the visuals of wine floats in drinks like New York sours. But the dry, tannic effects never suited me. Wine reductions, I discovered, let me soften those parching effects and still get the good flavor impacts of wine.

My first stab at a wine reduction cocktail is below. It made perfect sense to devote this drink to the Dead Boys' seminal classic "Sonic Reducer."

Sonic Reducer

- ½ oz Cinnamon Syrup
- 1 oz Grapefruit Juice
- 1 oz Red Wine Reduction
- 1 oz Watershed Four Peel Gin
- 1 oz Fruitlab Orange Liqueur
- 2 dashes Peychaud's Barrel Aged Bitters
- 1 orange rind spiral

Shake all ingredients with ice and double-strain into a chilled coupe. Using a channel knife, cut a long orange peel spiral and garnish.

Dutch Treat

One thing that many people don't know is that the Dutch invented gin. They assume it's an English spirit, but British soldiers actually brought it home from battlefields in Holland. England created a drier version and the rest is history.

The funny part is the slurs that the British soldiers used on the Dutch: "Dutch bargain" (a contract made when one is drunk), "Dutch concert" (when several tunes are played at the same time). Did you know you're really being a racist when you say "we're going Dutch" at a restaurant? It means you're making your guest pay their own tab.

So, I'd really be remiss excluding a Dutch gin or "Genever" cocktail. It's not everyone's cup of tea, being much sweeter and almost white whiskey-like. The juniper is there, but that's about it for the botanical flavors.

The drink below takes its name from the British slur meaning "a party where the host gets drunk before the guests." It attempts to balance the rather acquired taste of Genever with herbal and spicy notes.

Dutch Feast

 ¾ oz Oude or barrel-aged Genever gin

 ¾ oz dry orange curacao

 ¾ oz Cynar 70

 ¾ oz Byrrh

 2 dashes cinnamon bitters

 Star anise garnish

Stir all ingredients with ice in a mixing glass. Strain into a chilled coupe and rest the garnish on the drink surface.

Chapter 6: Rumbullion

Rum to me might just be the ultimate cocktail spirit. It's insanely versatile. Even higher grade rums are inexpensive unless they're double-digits in age. They blend exceedingly well with each other. And they gave us tiki. It's so damned good I got a "rum" bottle tattooed on my right hand.

Sadly, rum remains the unsung hero in most bars. Unless you're going to a tiki bar or destination cocktail bar, you'll likely find a shit brand of spiced rum (he mutters "Captain Morgan" under a cough) and an industrial grade silver rum wasting space in the well, waiting to be buried in fountain gun Coca-Cola.

It's quite sad that great rum brands have to jockey for bar shelf space against much lesser spirits. If this chapter convinces you to buy good brands of rum to help some outstanding producers in the retail market, I can die with a little less burning hatred for the squirrel-piss vodka makers that make me contemplate arson each day.

Rather than risk casting my words into an endless love song to rum, let's just get to the cocktails. I think we'll both be better for it.

Pocketing the Compass

Rum cocktails more often than not call for shaking, as they typically include citrus or other kinds of juice, or even coconut cream. I made it a quiet crusade to invent as many stirred rum cocktails as I could, as long as the flavor pairings made sense and passed the taste test. Below is one of those maiden voyages.

The Careless Navigator

- ¾ oz Tiki Lovers White rum (sub Bounty Dark or other rich white rum if not available)
- ¾ oz apple brandy or applejack
- ¾ oz Luxardo Sangue Morlacco
- ¾ oz Cynar
- 2 dashes Burlesque Bitters

Build all ingredients in a mixing glass. Add ice, stir and strain into a chilled coupe glass. Garnish with a Luxardo maraschino cherry on a skewer.

Wrong Season, Right Flavors

This one landed on a winter menu, though the rich, dark color and flavors felt more wintry. Regardless, when you drink it, I trust you'll enjoy it. The herbal notes of the Maurin make it pop. But if Cherry Heering is easier to find, it works well too.

Wrong 'Em, Boyo

- 1 oz fresh tangerine juice
- ½ oz Lemon Juice
- 1 oz Boysenberry Syrup
- 2 oz Diplomatico Anejo Rum
- ½ oz Maurin Quina or Cherry Heering
- Thyme and blueberry garnish

Shake all ingredients with ice and strain over a large format cube in a rocks glass. Lay berry on the cube. Rest thyme sprig on the edge of the glass.

The French Connection

Being in a stranglehold liquor control state like Ohio, it gets difficult to find proper cordial spirits that aren't sickly sweet rotgut, or anything outside garden variety flavors. Fortunately the French line of Giffard cordials is here. It uses all natural infusions, so you can use a flavor like Banane du Bresil without cloying sweetness. The portfolio also includes unusual flavors like lychee and rhubarb. The latter cordial inspired the cocktail below.

Rhu Morgue

- 1 oz Giffard Rhubarbe
- 1 oz Angostura White Oak Rum
- ¾ oz Falernum
- 1 oz Sudachi juice (lemon will work in its place)

Shake all ingredients with ice. Strain into a chilled coupe glass. Garnish with dried star anise.

Another French Connection

This book is making me realize something unknown before all of these recipes were compiled: too many of my drinks have names pertaining to France.

Though I pledge no real allegiance to the nation, I guess France just gives us so many great spirits: Chartreuse, cognac, Martinique rums, classic aromatized wines. And once again, Plantation rums from Pierre Ferrand.

Using these as a base, I sought to create a sort of proto-tiki version of the French 75. Ironically, the final result only resembled its inspiration in that it uses bubbly. This version takes its name from the year 1971, the year that British Naval sailors were given their final "tot" or "grog." This daily ration was commonly blended with lime juice and sugar. Ringing any bells?

French 71

- 1 oz Plantation 3 Stars Rum
- 1 oz Plantation O.F.T.D. Rum
- 1 Dash Bittercube Bolivar Bitters
- ½ oz fresh lime juice
- ½ oz orgeat
- Prosecco topper

Shake all but prosecco with ice and strain the mixture into a flute glass. Top with Prosecco, to taste. Using a channel knife or Y-peeler, peel a strip of rind from a lime and use this to garnish the drink.

Hive Mind

The springtime cocktail below was pollinated with a desire to use Greenbar's organic hibiscus cordial. The honey component of this drink compliments the floral notes nicely. The sweeter base spirits are balanced with fresh lime and a touch of pimento spice.

Queen Bee

- 1.5 oz Diplomatico Planas Rum
- ½ oz fresh lime juice
- ½ oz Maxime VS Cognac
- ¼ oz Bitter Truth Pimento Dram
- ½ oz Honey syrup
- ½ oz Greenbar Fruitlab Hibiscus cordial

Shake all ingredients with ice and strain over fresh ice in a snifter or tulip glass. Garnish with a fresh or dehydrated lime wheel.

The Hizzy of Angostura

Angostura is a household name when it comes to bitters. Originally hailing from Trinidad, the house of Ango has also introduced a stellar line of Caribbean rums and an amaro. Below is my tribute to the house that Angostura built.

Trinidad Shakedown

- 1 oz Angostura 7 Year
- 1.5 oz Lakewood Organic Dark Cherry Juice
- ½ oz Cardamaro
- ½ oz fresh lemon juice
- ½ oz Angostura Amaro
- 2 dashes Angostura orange bitters
- Candied ginger garnish on bamboo skewer

Shake all liquids with ice and then strain over fresh cubes in a snifter or tulip glass. For a spicier version, top with a short layer of Reed's Extra ginger beer.

All Aboard

Savory flavors play well with coconut in the foodie world, especially traditional Indian spices like curry and masala. These give a savory kick to the sweet date and mango in the rum cocktail below. While Indian brands of rum exist, they're a little harder to find in my experience. Just don't use Tiger Rum. It's so bad, even the flavors below probably couldn't bury it.

Express Kundalini

- 1 oz mango nectar
- 1 oz orange juice
- 2 oz Angostura White Oak Rum
- A dash of garam masala
- ½ oz Jallab (date) syrup
- Mint leaves and stalk, coconut chips

Muddle mint leaves and shake all with ice. Serve over ice in tulip glass. Garnish with mint stalk and coconut chips.

Preferred by 88 out of 88 Yakuza

I did at one time attempt a special evening's menu of Kill Bill cocktails. It didn't fully pan out. I managed two cocktails named after characters in the Japan chapter, one of which is below. Perhaps a full menu will unfurl in my mind eventually. Until then, enjoy this stirred rum number below, accented by Hakutsuru plum wine.

Johnny Mo

- 2 oz Tiki Lovers White Rum
- ½ oz dry orange curacao
- ¾ oz Hakutsuru plum wine
- ¼ oz Amaro Montenegro
- 2 dashes cinnamon bitters
- Persimmon cube garnish

Stir all ingredients with ice. Strain into a chilled coupe. Garnish with a dried or fresh persimmon cube on a skewer.

The Devil Made Me Do It

Rum in its early days was often called the "kill devil" due in no small part to its rough edges. In the spirit of the ancestral rum grog that meant to smooth these edges, the cocktail below adopts the traditional lime and sweetener, but pushes the limits with a bold mix of cardoon, blessed thistle, walnut, cardamom, clove, and ginger.

Kill Devil Blues

- 2 oz Mount Gay Eclipse Rum
- ½ oz lime juice
- ½ Royal Rose Cardamom Clove simple syrup
- ½ oz Cardamaro
- ½ oz Nux Alpina
- 1 dash Bittermens Krupnik Ginger Bitters

Shake all ingredients with ice and strain over a large format ice cube in rocks glass. Alternately, this can also be served up in a chilled coupe glass.

Autumn in New York

The cocktail below stirs together some lush, fall flavors, the most dominant of which is Barrow's Intense Ginger spirit from Brooklyn, NY.

Highway 78 Revisited

- ¾ oz Bounty Dark Rum
- ¾ oz Maggie's Farm Falernum spirit (sub Bitter Truth if needed)
- ¾ oz Tom's Foolery Applejack (or equivalent apple brandy/applejack)
- ¾ oz Barrow's Intense Ginger
- 2 dashes Woodford Reserve Cherry Bitters

Add all liquids into the mixing glass and stir with ice. Strain into a chilled coupe. Garnish with a fresh or dried lemon wheel.

Beyond the Sea

Perhaps bands with letters for names are the best muses. AC/DC inspired the main characters in Black Hawk Down and the Iron Man franchise. ELO inspired the Guardians of the Galaxy. And XTC inspired the following proto-tiki/tropical-style cocktail with a track appearing in the original song list on Skylarking.

Mermaid Smiled

- ½ oz pineapple juice
- ½ oz cinnamon clove syrup
- ½ oz mango nectar
- 2 dashes Bittermens Xocolatl Mole Bitters
- ½ oz Cantera Negra Cafe coffee spirit
- ¼ oz grapefruit juice
- 1.5 oz Myers's Dark Rum

Shake all ingredients with ice and strain over fresh ice in goblet or tulip glass. Garnish with fresh or dried mango or papaya.

The Captain's Mes(s)

Like the Highway 78 cocktail, this warming blend of rum and brandy has a herbal, spicy backbone. The lavish flavor of Punt e Mes vermouth gets a slightly earthy boost from Cynar.

The Winter Soldier

- ¾ oz Bounty Dark Rum
- ¾ oz apricot brandy
- ¾ oz Punt e Mes
- ¾ oz Cynar 70
- 2 dashes Old Forester Smoked Cinnamon Bitters
- Garnish: Luxardo cherry

Build all ingredients in a mixing glass. Add ice, stir, and strain into a chilled coupe glass. Garnish with a Luxardo cherry on a bamboo skewer.

My Cup Runneth Over(proof)

There are moments where you get rewarded for doing something stupid. Like trying to turn a light, refreshing Pimm's Cup into a Zombie. The cocktail on the opposite page is just such an instance. This one's like officiating a fever-dream wedding of Queen Elizabeth with Don the Beachcomber. Then they have a kid who turns out to be Jack the Ripper.

This one literally did win an award in 2017, at the Ohana cocktail competition in Lake George, NY. Sure it won 2nd place but against some fierce competition. I think it was the sheer audacity of uncivilizing a quaint English classic. Plus it's purple. Very purple. It turns out people love purple drinks. Make something purple at a bar and everyone who sees it says, "I'll have whatever that is."

Timm's Cup #3

½ oz fresh lemon juice
½ oz lime juice
½ oz honey syrup
1 oz Blackberry & Elderflower Pimm's
½ oz Solerno
¾ oz Wray & Nephew Overproof Rum
¾ oz El Dorado 5 Year Rum
¼ oz Hamilton Pimento Dram
Angostura Lemon, Lime and Bitters Soda

Shake all but soda with ice. Strain mixture over fresh ice in a tall Collins glass. Top with soda. Garnish with bruised mint sprig, fresh strawberry, and cucumber slice.

No, it's not Kraken

Like the prehistoric, volcanic landscape after which it's named, this cocktail may cause a mild case of the vapors. It gets peppery heat from habanero syrup, and spicy heat and aroma from curry.

Krakoa

½ oz Pope's Orange Habanero Syrup

½ oz fresh orange juice

1 oz Bacardi Cuatro (4 Year) Rum

1 oz Calvados

½ oz Cruzan Black Strap Rum

Orange curry powder and coconut chips

Shake all liquids with ice and then strain over crushed or pebble ice in a tulip glass. Sprinkle a light layer of curry powder and coconut chips on the surface.

Chapter 7: El Efecto Tequila

There are certain things you hear as a bartender that eventually make you lose patience and get mildly argumentative with guests. One of these things is "tequila turns me into a loco bandit without pants" or something to that effect.

My reply is that it's all in your head. Ethanol is ethanol. Studies have shown that all spirits have the same physical and chemical effects on everyone. You know why your scary Jekyll-to-Hyde potion turned you into a drunken maniac? It's because you did shots, amigo. Plain and simple.

Tequila seems to get this bad rap more often than other spirits and I just don't know why. Perhaps we can blame the bottled worm from days past (which actually was a gimmick with mezcal). Old wives' tales warned that the worm would make you hallucinate or turn you into a raging, feral bullfighter. This myth maybe latched onto tequila and stuck in people's psyche.

In reality, tequila and mezcal can make sublime cocktails. Tequila in particular pairs stunningly well with so many other flavors. You're doing yourself a disservice avoiding tequila drinks on misguided conceptions, whether these be about the taste, or the supposed ill effects the drinks might have.

Give at least one of the following drinks a whirl so I can say "I told you so."

Shock Value

When working at an American distillery, you typically make cocktails with the house spirits as your base, while your other options are usually cordials or other modifiers. This was not the case with tequila and mezcal, as they can only be made in Mexico. Hence, these spirits gave me a much wider breadth of creative freedom. The cocktail menu lauding Cleveland punk bands also provided ample inspiration. I made it a point to start with the lesser-known but very influential band The Electric Eels. I wanted this drink to have a slightly "shocking" bite, but still have well-balanced flavors. The sage, celery, and citrus provide the bite, while the honey and smooth silver tequila even out the initial sting on the palate.

Electric Eel

- 1 oz grapefruit juice
- ½ oz honey syrup
- ½ oz Del Maguey Vida Mezcal
- 1.5 oz Casa Noble Silver Tequila
- 2 dashes Bittermens Celery Shrub Bitters
- Sage leaves (for muddle and garnish)

Muddle 1–2 sage leaves with honey syrup and grapefruit juice in a shaker. Add the remaining ingredients and shake with ice. Double-strain over a large format cube in a rocks glass. Garnish with sage leaf.

Not Quite Hollywood

It's another purple cocktail, yes. This is just how my silly cocktail legacy unfurled. I didn't make it a point to create drinks that looked like the ones Gil Gerard drank on Buck Rogers in the 25th Century. It just happened. The more difficult part of this equation is coming up with jovial names that confess, "yeah, it's purple." This example gets its deep purple accent from Giffard's lovely blackberry cordial. Its namesake is a bawdy 1973 Australian sex comedy that, well, didn't exactly get positive reviews or oscar murmurs. My Australian friend loved the name, but oddly no one else questioned it.

Alvin Purple

- 1.5 oz Hakutsuru plum wine
- 1 dash Bittercube Corazon bitters
- 1.5 oz Espolon Silver Tequila
- ½ oz Giffard Creme de Mure
- ¾ oz agave simple syrup
- ½ oz fresh lime juice

Shake all ingredients but creme de mure with ice and strain into a chilled coupe glass. Slowly add creme de mure to form a purple layer at the bottom. Garnish with skewered blackberry.

Tequila, I've found, is so very versatile. You can often blend it into cocktails with spirits you would never assume pair well. The drink below is a perfect example. It combines silver tequila and spicy ancho cordial from Mexico with a quirky herbal Alpine spirit. And it works spectacularly.

The Alpine Standoff

- 1 oz Mi Campo Blanco Tequila
- ½ oz Genepy des Alpes
- ½ oz orgeat
- ½ oz lime juice
- ¼ oz Ancho Reyes Verde
- 1 dash Hellfire bitters

Shake all ingredients with ice. Strain over a large format cube in a rocks glass. Lay a lime wheel on top of the cube.

Estevez, Revisited

Writing recipes with tequila, you often fall into the abbreviation "repo" for "reposado." This almost always planted Iggy Pop's title track to "Repo Man" in my head. I'd argue this cult Alex Cox classic still holds up and gave Emilio Estevez his most relevant role.

The cocktail that sprung from this trigger reaction gets a mix of spice and berry flavors from blueberry amaro and mulberry molasses. This molasses and other eclectic syrups can be found very inexpensively at Middle Eastern markets. Visits to Cleveland's Middle Eastern neighborhoods gave me great inspirations for many cocktails.

Repo Man

- 1.5 oz Tres Agaves Reposado Tequila
- ½ oz Pasubio Vino Amaro
- ¼ oz Bitter Truth EXR or pimento dram
- ½ oz fresh orange juice
- ½ oz mulberry molasses

Shake all ingredients with ice, then strain over fresh ice in a Collins glass. For garnish, place a fresh jalapeno slice and orange peel on a bamboo skewer.

Double Bubble

I once worked at a Greek dining establishment with a unique cocktail bar. They had a drink menu unlike any I'd encountered and a great staff. Inspired by my time there, I'd made it a point to do a Greek-inspired cocktail that brought in native flavors of Greece. And I sure as hell wasn't going to use Ouzo. The recipe below only uses silver tequila as an apt base spirit. The traditional apricot, grape, and honey flavors come from other modifiers. The name is taken from the character "Nick the Greek" in Lock, Stock and Two Smoking Barrels. In cockney slang, this morphed "Greek" into "bubble and squeak," which then was shortened to simply "bubble."

Nick the Bubble

- 1.5 oz Espolon Silver Tequila
- ½ oz Rothman & Winter or Bitter Truth apricot liqueur
- ½ oz apricot nectar
- 1 oz Pavan
- ¼ oz honey syrup
- ½ oz grapefruit Juice
- Dried apricot and cherry garnish

Shake all ingredients with ice. Pour over fresh ice in a Collins glass. Garnish with dried apricot and brandied cherry on a skewer.

Stir It Up

I don't recall what happened here; this cocktail really should have been built on Jamaican pot still rum. It's a tribute to the first American singer-songwriter to pen and perform reggae hits. He was also the first non-Jamaican performer to record reggae in Kingston, Jamaica. I do honestly expect that an aged Jamaican rum would effectively substitute the anejo tequila in this recipe. I specify Altos as a solid producer that makes the most affordable anejo I know. The remaining parts draw flavors from Caribbean influences, particularly the pimento dram.

Johnny Nash

- 1.5 oz Altos Anejo Tequila
- 1 oz pineapple juice
- 1 oz fresh lemon juice
- ¾ oz fresh orange juice
- ¼ oz Bitter Truth Pimento Dram
- ½ oz vanilla syrup
- 10 drops Bittermens 'Elemakule Tiki Bitters

Shake all ingredients with ice and strain over fresh ice in a Collins glass. Garnish with a fresh or dehydrated lemon wheel.

Grab Your Thunder Buddy

Patron tequila deserves some props. This producer essentially sparked the craft tequila renaissance in the U.S. The Patron tiki cocktail movement in recent years also generated some very interesting creations. I enjoy their Citronge cordial line as well. At a very good cost, you can choose from orange, mango, lime, and pineapple spirits.

The cocktail below rests upon both Patron tequila and Citronge. It came about as part of a "tiki-la" (tequila-based tiki) cocktail menu I created. It will work with equivalent silver and orange spirits if Patron is not available. It will also help you relax in the midst of loud tropical thunderstorms as well.

Thunder Buddies

- 1 oz Patron Silver Tequila
- ¾ Patron Citronge Mango
- ¾ oz Don Ciccio & Figli Concerto Coffee Liqueur
- 3 oz coconut juice
- ¼ oz simple syrup
- ½ oz fresh lemon juice

Shake all ingredients with ice. Strain over crushed or pebble ice in a tall Pilsner glass. Add a dried or fresh mango garnish.

Seeing Red

Reading through many of the recipes in this book, you'll see that I often enjoy naming cocktails after films. And how could I not doff my hat to native Cleveland director P.T. Anderson. This recipe below might spark a full menu eventually. So don't go taking "Magnolia" or "Hard Eight" away from me.

This cocktail gets a unique flavor from blood orange juice, a sweeter herbal cordial, and barrel-aged red wine. The blood orange juice component limits it to December through April, though lemon juice can make it work year round.

There Will be Blood

- 1 oz Roca Patron Anejo
- ½ oz blood orange juice (fresh lemon juice can be substituted)
- ½ oz simple syrup
- ½ oz Greenbar Grand Poppy (or Aperol as a substitute)
- ½ oz bourbon barrel-aged red wine float

Shake all but the red wine with ice. Strain over a large format cube in a rocks glass. Slowly pour red wine onto the drink surface. Garnish with a fresh or dehydrated blood orange wheel.

Burning Down the House

Rum naturally built the house in which tropical cocktails live. Other spirits like gin, whiskey, and tequila only visit it occasionally and get the Murphy bed in the guest room. Well, I say there's room for everyone in this house. Especially tequila. Great things often happen when you limit yourself from using the naturally-expected spirit.

The cocktail below would surely work well with a proper gold rum with no artificial ingredients. The recommended reposado tequila gives it a more robust base.

Quemando tu Casa

- 1 oz Mi Campo Reposado Tequila
- ½ oz Demerara simple syrup
- ¼ oz Lemon Hart Blackpool Spiced Rum
- ½ oz Luxardo Maraschino cordial
- ¼ oz hibiscus syrup
- 1 oz fresh lemon juice

Shake all ingredients with ice and strain over fresh ice in a snifter or tulip glass. Rest a dried, edible hibiscus flower on the surface.

Deer Diary

I'm a pretty shameless fan of the Cazadores tequila line. It's probably the best I've come across at the overall price line. Each bottle features a portrait of a deer. The name "Cazadores," meanwhile, translates to "the hunters." Being a Clevelander, it seemed serendipitous to use this spirit in a cocktail named "The Deer Hunter." This 1978 dark drama was filmed in our city's Tremont neighborhood.

The Deer Hunter

- 2 oz Cazadores Reposado Tequila
- ½ oz Ancho Reyes Verde
- 1 oz fresh lime juice
- ½ oz pomegranate molasses
- Lime wheel and Amarena cherry flag garnish

Shake all ingredients with ice and strain into a chilled coupe. Shape flag garnish on skewer and lay inside the drink.

Touch of Aril

A handful of spirits companies make my job a lot easier. Washington DC-based Don Ciccio & Figli is just such a company. They make an incredible line of herbal, Italian-inspired cordials that quite often steal the show in a cocktail. The drink below is no exception.

This drink takes its name from the hotel at the U.S.-Mexico border in Orson Welles' Touch of Evil. It pairs native Mexican flavors like pomegranate, lime, and agave with the unique, sweet fennel spirit made by Don Ciccio & Figli.

Mirador Hotel

    1.5 oz Altos Silver

    ½ oz Don Ciccio & Figli Finocchietto Fennel Liqueur

    ¾ oz lime juice

    ½ oz agave syrup

    ½ oz POM Wonderful Pomegranate Juice and arils

Shake all liquid ingredients with ice and strain over fresh ice cubes in a Collins glass. Garnish with fresh pomegranate arils.

Things We Did on Grass

A friend in the industry connected me with Garden of Flavor, a small, organic cold-pressed juice producer. Her thought was that we could collaborate on some organic cocktails that used their unique juice blends. I looked at their array of juices, and some indeed leapt out as hugely promising cocktail ingredients. I formulated individual cocktails for about six different juices, which all worked well on their very first test runs.

The one juice I expected to fail or at least prove difficult was Grasshopper. Ingredients like kale, spinach and parsley sounded like a square peg for a round glass to me. I could not have been more wrong. This juice probably produced the best result in the whole endeavor. As far as I know, it can be found at most locations of Whole Foods.

Praying Mantis

    1.5 oz Espolon Blanco tequila

    ¾ oz fresh lime juice

    ½ oz rich simple syrup

    ½ oz Garden of Flavor Grasshopper juice

    ½ oz Tempus Fugit Kina l'Aero D'or Quinquina

Shake well with ice and serve over fresh ice in a rocks glass. Garnish with lime wedge and cilantro sprig.

Chapter 8: Whiskey Rebellion

The chapters of this book generally follow my learning path in mixology up to the current day. Fate decided that I wouldn't work at bars with a strong complement of whiskies until the latter days in that journey. God, I hate that word "journey." It sounds like I'm at some corporate retreat. Pick a better word while I keep typing.

So here we are, nearing the end of the book with one of the greatest and, frankly, hottest spirit categories of the moment.

The real joy I'll get from this chapter is enraging anyone that thinks it's sinful to shake drinks with bourbon. Or any other whiskey for that fact. If you have to validate your existence sharing neat pour photos on bourbon snob forums, suffice it to say you're missing out on great drink experiences. And more than likely a real social life.

Bourbon, rye, Scotch, and Irish whiskies can escalate the spirit cost of your cocktails if you use the better, more sought after brands in each category. But solid, inexpensive examples stand out in each group, too. For example, most bourbons in the Evan Williams (Heaven Hill) line cost less than $20 and make stellar cocktails.

It seems a bit naff writing only a short introduction for such a vast and robust class of spirits. But again, why delay getting to the bomb-ass cocktails for which you bought this fucking book?

Guns Blazing

It once came to pass that I needed a small menu of signature whiskey cocktails for a series of ongoing classes. This was fun. I wanted to really mix it up — not just offend all the whiskey purists, but put some truly unexpected stuff in the cocktails. "What?! There's a fishing lure and a severed human finger in my cocktail!" Okay, maybe not that weird.

Locally-made apple butter began appearing for fall in the area markets. This became the crux of the recipe I would create. I also yearned to play with bourbons that had secondary finishing in other types of spirit barrels. Perhaps it was providence that Amador Double Barrel hit the shelves around the same time.

The recipe that unfurled appears below. Since I was using Amador, I felt the name should refer to a renowned double-barrel shotgun. Research led me to the Fox Gun Company's "F Grade" shotgun that was made expressly for Teddy Roosevelt. The name and the rich flavor of this drink made it one of the most popular on the menu.

Teddy Roosevelt's Fox

- 1 heaping bar spoon apple butter
- ½ oz fresh lemon juice
- 1 oz Amador Double Barrel Bourbon
- 1 dash each Hellfire Shrub and Walnut bitters
- 1 oz Carcavelos or Madeira
- ¾ oz honey syrup
- Dried apple garnish

Shake all ingredients with ice and strain over a large format ice cube in a rocks glass. Lay dried apple garnish on top of the cube.

Staring Down Another Barrel

The next cocktail follows the odd progression of the same whiskey cocktail menu. The next whiskey I planned to fiddle with was Evan Williams Single Barrel Bourbon. It made sense to name this cocktail after a famous American single barrel rifle. The Winchester and its bizarre, haunted legend seemed the perfect fit.

The Sarah Winchester

- 1 oz Evan Williams Single Barrel Bourbon
- 1.5 oz bourbon barrel-aged Chardonnay
- ¾ oz fresh pink grapefruit juice
- ½ oz honey syrup
- ½ oz Amaro di Angostura
- Lemon peel and rosemary garnish

Shake all ingredients and strain over fresh ice in a Collins glass. Garnish with peel and rosemary.

Let's Be Neorealistic

Writing this book, I'm noticing a very overt fondness for Maggie's Farm Falernum cordial. It's a splendid high proof alternative to the far inferior brand Velvet. On the plus side, buying a bottle will let you make at least three recipes. Bitter Truth makes a good low proof falernum spirit as well. Velvet will work but make it your last resort.

Whichever you use, the sweet and spicy falernum spirit plays well with the herbal Chinato and less aggressive rye in this cocktail. Feel free to use the orange and aromatic bitters that you prefer. I originally made this with Cleveland-made bitters that are no longer on the market.

The Rye-cycle Thief

- 1.5 oz Rittenhouse Rye
- ¾ oz Maggie's Farm Falernum cordial (sub Bitter Truth or Velvet if unavailable)
- ¾ Cocchi Barolo Chinato
- 2 dashes orange bitters
- 2 dashes aromatic bitters

Stir all ingredients with ice in a mixing glass. Strain over a large format ice cube in a rocks glass. Skewer candied ginger and brandied cherry on a bamboo skewer to garnish.

I Menta Order Bourbon

This is a rare foray into hot holiday cocktails for me. It's not complicated, rather a good way to apply the intense sweet and herbal Branca Menta. A good unsweetened traditional Dutch cocoa balances well with the Branca Menta. But you can indulge your sweet tooth with a little simple syrup if needed.

Roman Holiday

- 1 oz Branca Menta
- 1 oz Redemption High Rye Bourbon
- 2–3 oz hot and blended Droste Cocoa
- 1 dash Bittermens Hellfire Shrub Bitters (optional)

Heat and prepare the cocoa separately. Add all ingredients in a glass or ceramic coffee mug. Garnish with a sprig of mint.

Next Link in the Daisy Chain

Daisy cocktails originated from Jerry Thomas' early cocktail recipes in 1876. They've budded here and there since then, but not enough in my estimation. A daisy is a simple cocktail with lemon or other citrus component, paired with a base spirit and a cordial spirit. My contribution to the legacy uses a very smooth micro-distilled bourbon and dry curacao.

Pushin' Up Daisies

- 2 oz New Holland Beer Barrel Bourbon
- ¼ oz dry orange curacao
- ½ oz Root 23 Pear Rosemary Syrup
- ½ oz orgeat
- ¾ oz lemon juice

Shake and double strain into coupe. Garnish with a sprig of rosemary.

The Beat from Badsville

The cocktail below was named in honor of The Cramps' first recorded drummer, Nick Knox. He was alive at the time it landed on the drink menu, but is sadly no longer with us. So it makes me happy that it will live on in print.

I think this exotic blend is a fitting tribute to a truly inimitable band. The spicy tamarind and ruby port make this as lush as red velvet leopard skin curtains.

Nick Knox

- ½ oz Tamarind Syrup (or Caged Heat Cocktail Syrup for a hot version)
- ½ oz fresh orange juice
- 1.5 oz Monkey Shoulder Scotch
- 2 dashes Angostura Orange Bitters
- ½ oz Ruby Port float
- Dried orange wheel garnish

Shake with ice. Strain over a large cube in a rocks glass. Top with Port float. Add a fresh or dehydrated orange wheel.

The Six-Demon Bag

Though bourbon is the base spirit in this drink, the Bigallet China-China steals the show with its unique blend of orange peels and spices. It's the most outstanding presence in a bouquet of fall flavors. I think Jack Burton would approve.

Bigallet Trouble in Little China-China

- 1.5 oz Redemption Bourbon
- 2 dashes Burlesque Bitters
- ½ oz Bigallet China-China
- ½ oz fresh lemon juice
- ½ oz cinnamon syrup
- Orchard apple cider to top

Shake all ingredients except cider with ice. Strain over fresh ice in a Collins glass, then top with cider. Garnish with a cinnamon stick.

Speyside Quest

This cocktail is a testament to the unique mixability of a 10-year single malt Scotch. You really don't often hear that. A bar owner once let me make a Blood & Sand with Macallan 12. It felt kinda dirty but really good at the same time.

Speyburn 10 works as a good cocktail base at a good cost, especially considering its age. It's almost too easy to pair it with honey, lemon, and ginger, almost like a good winter tea. You can give this drink a peppery kick with habanero bitters. This helps give it the kick of a "Scotch bonnet" Jamaican pepper, which gets its name from its shape (resembling a tam o'shanter hat).

Scotch Bonnet

- ½ oz fresh lemon juice
- ¼ oz Bitter Truth EXR
- ¼ oz honey syrup
- ¼ oz ginger syrup
- 1.5 oz Speyburn 10 Scotch
- 1 dash Scrappy's Habanero Firewater bitters (optional)
- Orange wedge punctured with 3 cloves to garnish

Shake. Strain over a large cube in a rocks glass. Garnish with punctured orange wedge.

Original Gangsters

When I was limited to Cleveland-related drink naming conventions, we did have some admittedly inspired ideas within those confines. One exemplary season, we created a "saints and sinners" theme, devoting each drink to either historic law enforcement figures or notorious criminals from our area. I naturally gravitated to the "sinners" segment.

The Cleveland area doesn't draw quite the legacy of gangsters that bigger cities did. But in the 1970s, our corner of Ohio gained the loving moniker "Bomb City USA" due to the mob's penchant for car bombs. Originally this was built with vodka (under duress), but the new formulation calls for the somewhat more explosive flavor of unaged rye whiskey.

Bomb City USA

- 1.5 oz Middle West Spirits White Rye Whiskey
- ½ oz fresh orange juice
- ½ oz dark brown simple syrup
- ½ oz Fruitlab Ginger cordial
- ¼ oz Nux Alpina walnut cordial
- 1 dash Bittermens Burlesque Bitters

Shake all ingredients with ice and strain over a large format cube in a rocks glass. Shave fresh nutmeg over the drink surface.

Waltzing Mathilde

I tend to gush over the outstanding producers of cordial spirits like Mathilde and Giffard. In a sea of artificially colored and flavored competitors, you can depend on these producers to make naturally infused spirits that provide important flavor options. I've gladly used Mathilde Peche in cocktails, but would sooner die than keep Paramount peach schnapps at arm's reach.

The drink below uses Mathilde Cassis or blackcurrant spirit. It's rather expensive for the 375 ml bottles in which it is sold. But it will go a long way. I thought it would be fun to pair this with red currant in the form of jam. Call it a "'jam session," if you will.

Alternating Currant

- 2 oz Old Forester 86 Bourbon
- 1 heaping bar spoon red currant jam or ½ oz red currant syrup
- ½ oz Mathilde Cassis (black currant) Liqueur
- ½ oz fresh key lime juice
- 2 dashes Bittermens Krupnik Honey Bitters

Shake all ingredients with ice. Strain over fresh ice in a rocks glass. Garnish with a lime peel and brandied cherry on a bamboo skewer.

Afternoon Delight

This was one of my earliest shrub cocktails. Shrubs are made with a blend of apple cider vinegar, a syrup, and usually some form of natural fruit juice. Pomegranate shrub plays delightfully well with bourbon alone. But this shrub gets a bit of added zest from blood orange and rhubarb spirits.

High Noon

- 1 oz pomegranate shrub (see Appendix for shrub recipe)
- 1.5 oz Redemption High Rye Bourbon
- ½ oz Solerno
- ¼ oz Amaro Sfumato Rabarbaro
- ½ oz maple syrup
- Cinnamon stick garnish

Stir all ingredients with ice and strain over a large format ice cube in a rocks glass. Using a lighter, smoke the end of a cinnamon stick and use this to garnish the drink.

Sexton and Violence

Among the gems in newer school Irish whiskies is Sexton Single Malt. It's aged in Jerez Oloroso sherry casks, which really sets it apart from any other Irish malts. It's also a deserving spirit for a cocktail dedicated to Danny Greene, Cleveland's most notorious Irish American mobster, who survived a staggering number of assassination attempts.

The cocktail below leans sweeter than most in my bag of tricks. Call it my amped-up Irish coffee. The egg white and mint aromatics give it an almost milkshake-like quality. The more intense sweetness of Velvet Falernum cordial works unusually well in this cocktail.

Danny Greene

- 1.5 oz Sexton Irish Whiskey
- ½ oz date syrup
- ½ oz Velvet Falernum spirit (or substitute brand)
- ½ oz Cherry Heering
- 1 oz cold brew
- 1 egg white
- 1 mint sprig to garnish

Crack an egg in half and carefully transfer the yolk between shells, letting the egg white drizzle into your shaker. Add the remaining ingredients and shake without ice vigorously for one minute. Add ice and shake again until the shaker frosts over. Strain the mix over a small amount of ice in a goblet. Add a mint sprig garnish.

(Snow)Blind Drunk

One fateful Tiki Tuesday, a guest from Columbus, Ohio visited my bar. It turned out that we had a shared affinity for the local spirits of the state capital, as well as the Grass Skirt Tiki Room, which is sadly no longer with us. He turned over the menu and challenged me to create a tiki-centric whiskey cocktail using Watershed Nocino, a local walnut spirit.

What you see below is a damn sight close to the challenge build that night. It had this odd gray hue, like the slushy winter streets of Cleveland. Suspend a skewered gooseberry over the surface as a metaphor for the cloud-concealed sun.

Blizzard of 77

- 1.5 oz Woodford Reserve Wheat Whiskey (or similar)
- ½ oz dry orange curacao
- ½ oz Nocino (Watershed Barrel Rested preferred)
- ¼ oz Tippleman's Double Spiced Falernum syrup
- ¾ oz fresh lemon juice
- ½ oz Giffard Orgeat
- 1 golden berry (gooseberry)

Shake all with ice and strain over fresh ice in a rocks glass. Garnish with a golden berry on a bamboo skewer.

Gravenstein's Monster

The tart, hazy effects of unfiltered Gravenstein apple juice balance nicely with the sweeter port and pear cordial in this cocktail. It's a nice fall cocktail though its ingredients bridge across the seasons. Blend in some orange bitters with the cocoa if you're feeling daffy.

Grave Disorder

- ½ oz Rothman & Winter Pear cordial
- 1.5 oz Old Forester Rye
- 1.5 oz Gravenstein Apple Juice
- ½ oz Sandeman or Warre's White Port
- 2 dashes Angostura Cocoa or Woodford Reserve Chocolate Bitters
- Dried pear garnish

Shake all but bitters and strain over a large format cube in a rocks glass. Garnish with rosemary sprig. Dash bitters over the cube. Lay a fresh or dehydrated pear slice on the cube.

Her Tannic Majesty's Request

Admittedly, wines are not my strong suit. The only ones that I've warmed up to are those aged in other types of spirit barrels. I've also found that their rounded flavors work quite well in cocktails. The recipe below melds the relative dryness of white wine and white grapefruit with wheated bourbon and sweet, herbal amaro. It's quite similar to the Sarah Winchester if you're fond of that concoction.

The White Queen

- 1 oz Maker's Mark Bourbon
- 1 oz Cooper & Thief Tequila Barrel-Aged Chardonnay
- ½ oz blanco (sweet white) vermouth
- ¾ oz Yuzu juice (sub lemon or white grapefruit if needed)
- ½ oz agave syrup
- ½ oz Averna
- Dehydrated or fresh orange wedge and cherry (such as Luxardo or Amarena)

Shake all ingredients with ice. Strain over fresh ice in a Collins glass. Garnish with orange wedge and brandied cherry.

Bittersweet Symphony

A cup of Cafe Du Monde Coffee ranks among those little indulgences one cannot pass up in New Orleans, much less the heritage cocktails in the same blast radius. The spirit-forward blend below aims to capture some of those nutty, chicory coffee flavors. If you'd prefer a version with more cherry, orange, and dried fruits, use Bittercube Trinity Bitters in place of the Chicory Pecan.

Concerto Macabro (aka Hangover Square):

- 1.5 oz Woodford Reserve Bourbon
- ¾ oz Nux Alpina
- ¾ oz Don Ciccio Concerto Coffee Liqueur
- 2 dashes El Guapo Chicory Pecan Bitters
- Orange peel and cherry garnish

Stir all ingredients with ice in a mixing glass. Strain into a chilled coupe. Twist the orange peel over the glass to express the oils. Coil up the peel around a cherry on a bamboo skewer as garnish.

Stop Mincing About and Drink

A considerable number of this cocktail were ordered when I put it on a special winter holiday menu. I hope this validates its very odd inspiration.

I don't cherish many holiday memories. But I do fondly recall the aroma of mincemeat pie: the raisins, brandy-steeped dried fruits, apple, spices. To me, it made sense to create a relaxing liquid version of this seasonal delight. The recipe below calls for some Cleveland area spirits, but it will work with equivalent spirits from other producers.

Let Me Stare into those Mince Pies

- 1.5 oz Tom's Foolery Wheat Whiskey
- ½ oz Tom's Foolery Applejack
- ¾ oz fresh orange juice
- ½ oz Giffard orgeat syrup
- 1 heaping bar spoon Robertson's mincemeat
- 2 dashes El Guapo Holiday Pie or Fee Brothers Walnut Bitters (optional)

Muddle the mincemeat with syrup and juice in a shaker. Add the remaining liquids and shake with ice. Strain mix over fresh ice in a rocks glass. Garnish with an orange wedge and cinnamon stick.

Chapter 9: Polynesian Remedies

Based on my experience, tiki cocktailing separates the children from the adults in our industry. Or perhaps it's the sane from the insane. The first proper cocktails I ever made were tiki drinks, and now it's how I make a living. So drop my name tag in that "insane" bucket, I guess.

Classic and signature drinks at better bars typically call for 4–6 ingredients, tops. Surpass this and you'll have a hard time getting bespoke drinks up to everyone's lips. The Yelp reviews will whine, "I waited 30 minutes for a drink!!!" The experienced among us know this is to be expected with good cocktails, and to order with a degree of foresight and patience.

The ratio of your garden variety cocktail bars versus tiki bars might be 30 or more to one in a major city, and that's if it's fortunate enough to have a tiki bar. It's a niche demanding a commitment to say the very least. An owner must go over the top on decor alone. Any location must be dressed head to toe in rattan, bamboo, carvings, and exotic art. And if owners want a custom cocktail tiki mug, they'd better be willing to sell off some organs to make this happen.

The bigger rub is the number of ingredients in your average tiki drink. Compared to your other modern cocktail bars, tiki bars usually produce cocktails where 4–6 ingredients are the simple ones. Tiki drinks like 1934 Zombies and the classic Jet Pilot demand 9–10 ingredients. And some of those ingredients must be made in-house with multiple other ingredients.

Working in a tiki bar now, I am pretty damned proud to say that I do. Hell, I respect anyone who can line up six shakers and simultaneously measure off different drinks in each one. I've seen tiki bartenders line up 12 shakers and do the same thing with double the ingredients, all working from muscle memory. I doff my fez to you, comrades.

Tiki at home, on the other hand, offers the luxury of a more relaxed pace. Friends are impressed enough at the effort and shouldn't judge you if you read the recipes from a book. They'll also discover that tiki cocktails are quite the opposite of "girlie drinks;" they are complex blends of spirits and tropical ingredients that usually require you to leave your car at the bar.

This is where I insert an impassioned "thank you" to Uber and Lyft.

Tiki drinks lean on a core regimen of ingredients, including a substantial range of rums, citrus, and tropical fruit juices, select cordial spirits, and syrups like falernum, orgeat, and passion fruit. These cross-pollinate so many different recipes because even the staple spirits and ingredients can barely fit behind the same bar.

With this in mind, it's a heightened challenge to invent new tiki drinks that don't resemble drinks originally invented across decades of the genre. This makes me especially proud of my tropical creations. These also pay tribute to my first love in cocktailing. Truth be told, I would not have ever bartended or written this book without tiki's unexpected arrow piercing my heart many years ago.

Gorillas in the Mist

Not for the faint of heart, my first signature tiki creation boasts bold flavor and a healthy complement of spirits. If blackstrap molasses are not your thing, just turn the page now.

This drink also pushes banana flavor to the limits of my comfort zone. It's fortunate that proper, naturally-infused banana spirits have hit the market. I love a good Planet of the Apes cocktail at the tiki bar. But I'd sooner fellate a banana on the jumbotron in Times Square than use 99 Bananas in any cocktail with my name on it.

Gorilla Panic!!!

- 1 oz Cruzan BlackStrap
- 1 oz Western Reserve Distillers Silver Rum
- ½ oz demerara syrup
- ½ oz fresh lime juice
- ¾ oz Giffard Banane du Bresil
- 2 dashes Bittermens 'Elemakule Tiki Bitters
- ¼ oz Bitter Truth EXR

Shake all ingredients with ice and pour directly into a mai-tai (large rocks) glass or comparable size tiki mug. Add a banana chip garnish.

How about a Hawaiian Punch...er, Swedish...

Kronan Swedish Punsch is one of the most alluring spirits I've ever used. And yet it's such a sleeper. Four out of five guests would inquire about what it is. It's a national drink of Sweden, made with spices and both East and West Indies rums. It makes over 50 classic cocktails. Still, no one knows what it is.

The concoction below is my love letter to Swedish Punsch.

Five-Finger Death Punsch

- 1 oz Bounty White Rum
- ½ oz Hamilton 151
- ¾ oz Kronan Swedish Punsch
- ½ oz cinnamon syrup
- ¼ oz fresh lime juice
- 2 oz Garden of Flavor Appleade (substitute unfiltered, natural apple juice or orchard cider if needed)

Shake and strain over a large format cube in a rocks glass or tiki mug. Garnish with a fresh or dehydrated lime wheel.

Rocket from the Tomb

Early in my days as a paid bartender, I quickly embraced Brian Miller's "Gantt's Tomb" cocktail. This was his liquid poem to Ernest Raymond Beaumont Gantt, known better as Don the Beachcomber. Miller's resume is unparalleled (Death & Company, Pegu Club, Pouring Ribbons, and the Polynesian). So whenever he tried something new, it would get my attention.

Moving forward, I invented my own versions of "the tomb" until it blossomed into what you see below. I inscribed my tomb, however, with the name of Stiv Bators. Drink enough of these and you just might meet him on the other side.

Stiv's Tomb #2

- ½ oz fresh lemon juice
- ½ oz turbinado simple syrup
- 1.5 oz Santa Cruz Organic Apricot Mango Nectar
- 1 oz Pusser's Blue Label Rum
- 1 oz Templeton Rye
- ½ oz Plantation O.F.T.D. Overproof Rum
- ¼ oz Hamilton Pimento Dram

Shake all with ice and strain over crushed or pebble ice in a hurricane glass or tiki mug. Garnish with pineapple leaves and mango cube on a skewer.

More Purple Shit

One of the aforementioned Brian Miller's experiments was to work with ube-infused simple syrup. This purple sweet potato has an intense floral, almond-like sweetness and a deep violet color. My forebear was really on to something, as proven by my own ube undertaking. Just a few drops of natural ube extract has an enormous impact on raw sugar simple syrup.

The recipe I created calls for Pomelo juice. It's a southeast Asian ancestor of grapefruit and has a brighter, less bitter flavor. The fruits are very large and heavy and have thicker rinds. They do not yield as much juice but the flavor is lovely and distinct. If making this cocktail en masse, I'd suggest instead using 100% natural pink grapefruit juice.

Inu Poni

- 2 oz Diplomatico Planas Rum
- ½ oz ginger syrup
- ½ oz Ube simple syrup
- 1 oz Pomelo juice
- 2 dashes Bittermens 'Elemakule Tiki Bitters

Shake all ingredients with ice. Pour over fresh ice in a Collins glass or tiki mug. Garnish with a pineapple leaf and skewered pineapple cube.

Storm Warning

This tropical blend will dash the careless against the rocks. It aspires in strength to the notorious 1934 zombie. Don't say I didn't warn you.

Tropic Thunder

- 1.5 oz Bounty Spiced Rum
- ¾ oz Worthy Park Rum-Bar Silver
- ¾ oz Cruzan Black Strap Rum
- ¾ oz Fruitlab Hibiscus cordial
- 1 oz fresh lime juice
- 1 oz fresh orange juice

Shake all ingredients with ice and strain over new ice in a pilsner glass or tiki mug. Garnish with lime and orange wedges on a bamboo skewer.

Ain't it Fun

The greatest joy of the CLE punk tribute cocktail menu was actually not the response to the cocktails themselves, but the guests that recognized the musicians after which the drinks were named. Patrons would tell us they know surviving members or "that guy slept on my couch!"

Perhaps the best moment was a visit from a local artist who knew the Dead Boys. He got a first look at the menu and immediately texted a picture to Cheetah Chrome, legendary guitarist of the Dead Boys. I regret that I didn't have a menu and a Sharpie when I briefly met Cheetah some years back.

Cheetah Chrome

- ¾ oz fresh lemon juice
- ½ oz orgeat
- 2 oz Plantation Stiggins' Fancy Pineapple Rum
- ½ oz Giffard Lichi-Li (Lychee) cordial
- 2 dashes El Guapo Polynesian Kiss Bitters
- Lemon peel and Luxardo cherry garnish

Shake all liquids with ice. Double-strain into a chilled coupe. Skewer lemon peel around cherry on a bamboo skewer and garnish.

Krampus Kooler

Literally translating to "dark Christmas," the cocktail below will actually be a pleaser year round. The dark, tart cherry juice simply helped settle on a name when it was added to a holiday cocktail menu. Perhaps I should have named it "elf blood."

Pouli Kalikimaka

- 1.5 oz Patron Reposado Tequila
- ¾ oz Patron Citronge Mango cordial
- 1 oz Lakewood Organic Dark Cherry Juice
- ½ oz fresh lime juice
- ½ oz Pimento Dram
- ¼ oz falernum

Shake all ingredients with ice and strain over crushed ice or pebble ice in a snifter or tulip glass, or a tiki mug. Garnish with lime wedge and cranberries.

Aloha from Hell

I once worked at a bar where the visionary manager cancelled the tiki program for the winter. When you live on the shoreline of lake-effect blizzards, when the fuck else would you want to pretend you're in the tropics? Is it any wonder the bar locked its doors several years ago? No one liked that manager. It wasn't just me. If you're reading this, you know who you are.

The drink below reminds us that refreshing and well-crafted tropical drinks are never more important than during winter. When a season of crippling storms can dump a foot of snow before sundown, this well-balanced, long-distance drinker will let you hula well into the night.

Kumu Hula

- 1 oz Diplomatico Planas Rum
- 1 oz Pavan
- ½ oz passion fruit nectar
- ½ oz fresh lemon juice
- 1 dash Angostura bitters

Shake all ingredients with ice and strain into a chilled coupe glass.

Slane in Vain

NYC's Dead Rabbit Grocery & Grog, a very Irish-focused craft cocktail bar, announced they intend to release their own signature tiki mug. That announcement landed on social media in the middle of a drunken whirlwind. When I came to the following day, I found this scribbled on a note in my pocket with the barely legible reminder "buy rabbit mug."

Gaelic Grog

- 1.75 oz Slane Irish Whiskey (or Dead Rabbit Irish Whiskey if you can find it)
- ½ oz Velvet Falernum spirit
- ½ oz Copper & Kings Craft Brandy
- ½ oz fresh lime juice
- ½ oz cinnamon syrup
- 1 dash Fee Brothers Walnut Bitters

Shake all ingredients with ice and strain over fresh ice in a Mai Tai (large rocks) glass or comparable size tiki mug. Garnish with a mint sprig.

Deutsch Treat

Anyone tuned into tiki knows Sven Kirsten. A German expat now living on the west coast, he penned many seminal books on tiki culture and architecture and helped the scene regain steam over the past couple decades. One evening at a friend's home tiki bar, I frankensteined together a liquid love letter to Sven.

This friend's bar offered up a weird amalgam of spirits, some of which were German. These included Kummel, a sweeter caraway spirit, and Kirschwasser, a dark German cherry spirit. The woodruff syrup ended up in a later iteration I made with ingredients in my own home bar. This unique sweetener is traditionally blended with Berliner weisse beer in Germany.

I recommend creating a Krautrock/Exotica playlist to enjoy in the background of this oddly pleasing German/tropical hybrid cocktail.

Kaiser Kai

- 1 oz Combier Kummel (another brand of kummel or aquavit will also work)
- 1 oz Myers's Dark Jamaican Rum
- ½ oz fresh lemon juice
- ½ oz Kirschwasser (Cherry Heering will work as a substitute)
- ½ oz woodruff syrup
- ¼ oz orgeat
- 2 dashes Fee Brothers Walnut Bitters

Shake all liquids with ice and then strain over fresh ice in a rocks glass or tiki mug. Garnish with lemon peel and a Luxardo cherry on a bamboo skewer.

Chapter 10: Stranger Than Paradise

Consider this chapter the final resting place of "strange" recipes that I just cannot categorize more effectively. "Here lies all of Tim's clever drinks that he was just too stupid or tired to put under a better chapter title."

It's also the resting place of any recipes that forced me to use vodka. Just so I could live with myself as a bartender, all of these use vodkas with natural fruit or vegetable infusions. You can make each infusion at home using store-bought items. Any recipes built on brandy, cordials, or other oddball spirits are also here in this chapter.

Despite my lack of effort building this chapter, I say without reservation that I'm proud of the drinks and they all taste really fucking good.

The Water of Life

Imagine Scandinavia had its own version of gin. Well, it sort of does: "akvavit" or aquavit, meaning "water of life." The principal botanical isn't juniper, it's caraway seed or dill. Open a bottle and it won't smell like a pine forest, it will have the aroma of rye bread. Like gin, it can have any number of other botanicals. Often these include fennel, lemon peel, and coriander.

Even with the simplest of builds, aquavit makes amazing savory cocktails. It also provides a useful application for otherwise pointless vodka. A simple infusion gives you a pretty dazzling aquavit. In fact, there's an easy recipe in the Appendix of this very book. Damn hell, that alone is worth the price of admission.

Maybe it's the ¼ fraction of Swede in my genetic makeup, but I love aquavit. If you don't wish to make your own, Norden Distillers in Detroit makes lovely unaged and cask-aged aquavit with a complex botanical build. Several other microdistillers in Minnesota and greater Michigan also make great examples of the spirit.

Here's two recipes you can try. Both include some form of honey, which blends nicely with the rye notes of the spirit.

An Italian Werewolf in Norway

1.5 oz Aquavit
½ oz Pasubio Vino Amaro
½ oz fresh lemon juice
½ oz honey syrup
Star anise garnish

Shake all ingredients with ice. Strain into a chilled coupe glass. Garnish with anise.

Voice of the Beehive

1.5 oz Aquavit
1 oz grapefruit juice
½ oz Cherry Heering
½ oz Barenjager
¼ oz Falernum
2 dashes Krupnik herbal honey bitters

Shake all ingredients with ice. Strain over a large format cube in a rocks glass. Garnish with a cherry and lemon peel on a bamboo skewer.

Winter Warmer

This cocktail joins sweet, nutty flavors with carefully selected botanicals. I would recommend using an organic, corn-based vodka to infuse the cardamom (see the Appendix for guidance). The tiny amount of saffron water in this mix gives the drink a warm orange glow and a floral aroma. You can find saffron water at most Middle Eastern grocers very affordably.

Space Heater

- ¾ oz Giffard Creme de Cacao
- ¾ oz fresh lemon juice
- ¼ oz Fratello Hazelnut cordial
- ¾ oz brown sugar syrup
- ¾ oz cardamom infused vodka
- 2 drops Saffron Water

Shake all liquids with ice and strain over a large format cube in a rocks glass. Lay a single sage leaf on top of the cube.

Use your Infusion

I keep my distaste for vodka no secret. However, this easy fig infusion makes quite a versatile, unique, and flavorful spirit. The spirit also draws a deep brown color from the figs. Below are two recipes you can make using the fig-infused spirit. Do you take tea or coffee?

Tea - Mr. Brownstone

- 2 oz fig-infused vodka
- 1 oz black tea
- ½ oz Copper & Kings Craft Brandy
- ½ oz date syrup
- 2 dashes orange bitters
- Dried fig on skewer for garnish

Stir all ingredients with ice. Strain over fresh ice cubes in a snifter. Garnish with a dried fig.

Coffee - A Cold Day in Hell

- ¾ oz cold brew concentrate (Scoot Cold Brew in Cleveland is recommended)
- ¾ oz Averna Amaro
- ¾ oz Fratello Hazelnut or Frangelico Liqueur
- ¾ oz fig-infused vodka
- 2 dashes Bittermens Hellfire Shrub Bitters
- Espresso coffee bean garnish

Stir all ingredients with ice. Strain mixture over a large format cube in a rocks glass. Lay a single espresso bean on top of the ice cube.

Cran-scary

Proper, natural infusion gives vodka a higher purpose — good flavor. That too is the core purpose of cocktail culture. It also reminds us that flavors normally considered pedestrian, like cranberry, can take on higher importance when carefully blended with other flavors. Consider too that cranberry-infused gins are slowly becoming more common.

Both cranberry-infused gin and vodka gave me creative fodder throughout the fall and winter seasons. I discovered that these paired the herbal sweetness of Yellow Chartreuse, muddled lemon, and fresh rosemary really well. The cocktail below is the result.

Crash and Burn

- ½ oz dark sugar syrup
- 2 oz Cranberry-infused vodka
- ½ oz Yellow Chartreuse
- Rosemary (shake and garnish) and fresh cranberries
- Pieces of diced, fresh lemon

Muddle rosemary leaves, cranberries, and lemon with syrup in the shaker. Add spirits with ice and shake. Strain over fresh ice in a Collins glass. Using lighter, smoke one end of rosemary sprig and garnish. Add cranberries and lemon peel on a bamboo skewer.

Cocktail from The Black Leather Lagoon

You may have noticed a number of cocktails in this book call for jallab or date syrup. It's a staple at Middle Eastern markets at a very low cost, though you can also find smaller, more expensive jars at high-end grocers too. It's fantastic to mix with, especially in fall and winter cocktails. And as you see below, it also lets you lay another offering at the altar of The Cramps.

This build calls for Armagnac, which can be spendy and difficult to find. So a respectable brandy can work in its place.

A Date with Elvis

¼ oz fresh lemon juice

½ Jallab (date) syrup

2 oz Armagnac Castarede

½ oz Rothman & Winter or Bitter Truth Apricot cordial

2 dashes cranberry bitters

Shake all with ice and strain into chilled coupe glass. Garnish with a dried date on a bamboo skewer.

Throw Vodka from the Train

My ongoing crusade against vodka has led me to a fascinating array of alternate clear spirits like Japanese Shochu. This spirit can be made from a broad spectrum of plants including rice, barley, sweet potatoes, buckwheat, brown sugar, chestnut, sesame, or carrots.

The drink below is made with "imo" or sweet potatoes, having a sweeter and floral character. The citrus and brown sugar components balance out the slightly funky, sake-like quality of the Shochu.

Bar Car on the Orient Express

¾ oz Solerno blood orange cordial

1.75 oz Ikkomon Shochu

4 dashes Regan's orange bitters

½ oz brown sugar syrup

½ oz Yuzu juice (or substitute freshly squeezed lemon juice)

Shake and serve in chilled coupe glass. Twist orange peel over the surface to express the citrus oils, then coil on a bamboo skewer as a garnish.

The Art of Drinking

I should have done more cocktails honoring Pere Ubu just for their musical influence alone. I met frontman Dave Thomas once and his cranky vitriol quite resembled my own. He probably hates vodka too. At least I hope so.

Below is my pear-shaped homage to Dave and his merry string of misfits. And much like their eclectic sound, this has an odd but well-balanced mix of spirits: South American pisco, pear cordial, Italian dry vermouth, and an artichoke amaro.

Pear Ubu

- 1 oz Rothman & Winter or Mathilde Pear Liqueur
- ½ oz Carpano Dry Vermouth
- ½ oz Cynar 70
- 1 oz Macchu Pisco or Barsol Pisco
- 2 dashes Chocolate bitters
- Dried or fresh pear garnish

Stir all ingredients with ice. Strain into a chilled coupe. Garnish with pear.

Drinks the Lord Taught Us

I promise, this is my last Cramps tribute cocktail. Maybe. At least in this book, anyways. If you've ever watched Poison Ivy Rorschach play a cherry red hollowbody guitar, you'd know why she deserves a devotional cocktail. And probably a gold statue.

In terms of flavor, the cocktail is almost more of a tribute to the Batman villainess of the same name. It's a strange, savory amalgam of plant flavors, the most forward of which is carrot ginger turmeric juice. The sweeter butternut squash, brown sugar, and hazelnut flavors balance this out, while the sage garnish gives the drink a sharp plant aroma.

Poison Ivy

- 2 oz R.W. Knudsen Carrot Ginger Turmeric Juice
- ½ oz fresh lemon juice
- 1.5 oz Butternut squash-infused vodka (see Appendix for guidance)
- ½ oz Frangelico
- 2 sage leaves

Muddle a sage leaf with lemon juice in a shaker. Add spirits, carrot juice, and ice. Shake briskly and then strain into a chilled coupe. Garnish with sage leaf.

The Godlike Power of Cocktails

The Pagans and many splinter bands put a huge impact in the indie music world we know today. Their influence can be traced through a dynasty of musicians, some of which are still active. Being that their namesake hailed a centuries-old movement refuting religion and authority, I aimed to make a drink using flavors from the Pagan heyday.

The fig maple shrub is the centerpiece of the cocktail. You can find guidance on shrubbery in the Appendix, along with steps to make the cranberry spirit infusion. The elements giving you the most wiggle room are the orange, cinnamon, and ginger spirit.

Pagan's Progress

- ½ oz fig maple shrub
- ½ oz fresh orange juice
- ½ cinnamon syrup
- 1.5 oz Cranberry-infused vodka
- ½ oz Fruitlab Ginger cordial
- 2 fresh cranberries

Shake all liquids with ice and strain over fresh ice cubes in a goblet. Garnish with cranberries on a skewer.

Kronan the Barbarian

The Rumbullion chapter of this book already testifies to my love of Kronan Swedish Punsch. However, I created a couple more cocktails where this spirit wasn't pitted against other forms of rum. The two below blend Kronan with different forms of gin and other cordials.

Stockholm Syndrome

- ¾ oz lingonberry syrup (or a heaping bar spoon of lingonberry jam)
- ¾ oz Plymouth Sloe Gin
- ¾ oz Kronan Swedish Punsch
- ¾ oz fresh lime juice
- Swedish fish to garnish

Shake all liquids with ice and strain into a chilled coupe glass. Place Swedish fish on a bamboo skewer to garnish.

Halo Effect

- ¾ oz organic white grape juice
- ¾ oz New Holland Knickerbocker Gin
- ¾ oz Kronan Swedish Punsch
- ¾ oz Cherry Heering
- Skewered lime peel and brandied cherry garnish

Stir all liquids with ice in a mixing glass. Strain into a chilled coupe. Stick lime peel around the cherry and stick on a bamboo skewer to garnish.

Appendix

The farewell section of this book provides guidance on some of the handmade components called for in drink recipes. All of these can be found through commercial producers, but you may prefer to make these yourself, if not for cost savings, perhaps bragging rights. The segments that follow include:

- Aquavit
- Vodka infusions
- Shrub mixes
- Syrups
- Wine reductions

Homemade Aquavit Recipe

As mentioned in the cocktail recipes, outstanding aquavits are on the market in most states. I like to try artisan producers' expressions simply because they each have distinct botanical builds. The five-ingredient recipe below lets you make a basic but flavorful version that will work for all the aquavit cocktails in this book.

Aquavit Infusion: To convert a single bottle of vodka

Ingredients:

    1 sprig fresh dill

    Three to four 2-inch strips of lemon peel, without pith

    1 teaspoon caraway seeds

    3 pods star anise

    ½ teaspoon fennel seed

Directions:

- Put the vodka, dill, and lemon zest in a large, sealable glass jar.
- Seal and shake, then let steep at room temperature for one day.
- Remove and discard the lemon zest and dill.
- Place the caraway seeds, star anise, and fennel seed in cheesecloth and tie the cloth shut.
- Place the dry botanicals into the infused vodka. Let steep at room temperature for an additional 2 days. For stronger flavor, continue to steep for up to two weeks. When the desired flavor is achieved, remove the cheesecloth.
- Store aquavit at room temperature or in the refrigerator for up to 6 months.

Vodka Infusions

This section gives you the basic steps to make the infusions specified in the cocktail recipes (fig, cranberry, butternut squash, and cardamom). But the same ideas apply for any type of infusions you might want to make.

Infusing vodka simply means to steep fruit, spices, or other plants in the spirit for a set amount of time. The longer the infusion material rests in the spirit, the more flavor and color the spirit absorbs.

Small spices like cardamom seeds are best sealed in cheesecloth before steeping. This makes it easier to steep and then remove when it's done. Alternately you can just place the seeds or other material into the spirit, then pour it through a mesh strainer when you finish steeping. This also strains out fruit seeds like strawberry or fig seeds that separate from the fruit.

The basic process is as follows:
- If using berries, fruits, or vegetables, cut them into small cubes or parts so that the spirit can absorb the flavor from below the plant skin.
- If using spices with thick shells like cardamom, using a rolling pin, crack the seed shells.
- For butternut squash: Spread the cubed plant pieces on a baking sheet and coat them with brown sugar. Bake until the cubes are cooked through and soft.
- Empty the vodka from the bottle into a large, sealable jar and save the bottle. Repeat if infusing multiple bottles at once.
- Place the prepared plant material into the vodka.
- Routinely taste the infusion spirit until it has the desired taste. (Note: Most infusions only take a couple of days, but the longer you steep, the more flavor you get.)
- Attaining the desired flavor, separate or strain the infusion material from the spirit and return the spirit to the original bottle(s). You may end up with a little less than before, as fruits and other plants absorb some of the spirit.

Shrub Mixes

Like infusions, shrub mixes typically follow a similar process. At a minimum, a shrub will be a blend of vinegar (apple cider most commonly) and some form of syrup (simple, maple, etc.). More complex versions will blend in some form of natural juices and/or herbs. For a much fuller resource on the subject, seek out Shrubs: An Old-Fashioned Drink for Modern Times by Michael Dietsch.

Commercially-produced shrub mixes can also be found online or at gourmet outlets. It's easy enough and less expensive, however, to make your own. Here are the instructions for the fig maple and pomegranate shrub mixes called for in this book.

Fig Maple Shrub

Ingredients: For a single batch (a blender should hold up to 2)
- 1 pint fresh purple figs with stems removed
- 2 cups warm water
- ½ cup apple cider vinegar
- 2 cups maple syrup

Directions:
- Add the ingredients into the blender pitcher.
- Blend the mix until all solids can be heard to break up and consistent liquid vortex appears in the blender.
- Pour mix through a large conical mesh strainer into a storage container. You may have to unclog the strainer.
- Taste mixture for acidity. If needed, add water or syrup, stir and re-sample.
- Place container in the refrigerator.

Pomegranate Shrub

Ingredients:
- 3 cups 100% pomegranate juice
- 1.5 cups apple cider vinegar
- 1.5 cups raw unrefined sugar

Directions:
- Add the sugar and water into a saucepan and heat on low. Stir until sugar dissolves.
- Add dissolved simple syrup and pomegranate juice into a large mixing vessel and stir thoroughly.
- Using funnel, pour mix into a serving bottle and then refrigerate.

Syrups

Unless you're making a more complex syrup like orgeat or falernum, most syrup mixes can be made easily at home, and often more cheaply. Here are easy instructions for cinnamon syrup and grenadine, along with guidance for homemade orgeat and falernum (should you choose to make them rather than buy them).

Cinnamon syrup

Ingredients:
- 1 tsp vanilla extract
- 1 tsp cinnamon
- 1 cup brown sugar
- 1 cup hot water
- 3–4 cloves

Directions:
- In a kitchen container, mix all spices and liquids with a spoon until all parts are dissolved and even in color.
- Add cloves to the mixture.
- After steeping overnight, remove cloves.
- Using a funnel, add to serving bottles.

Grenadine

- Mix equal parts simple syrup with 100% pomegranate juice in a kitchen container.
- Add a teaspoon of rose water.
- Using funnel, fill serving bottles as needed.

Orgeat

Ingredients:

    2 cups blanched almonds

    1.5 cups sugar

    1.25 cups water

    1 ounce brandy

    ½ teaspoon orange flower water

Directions:
- Finely grind almonds. Set aside.
- Heat the sugar and water in a pot over medium heat and stir until sugar dissolves. Boil for 3 minutes, then add the ground almonds.
- Simmer for another three minutes, then slowly increase the temperature to medium-high. Just before it starts boiling, remove the pot from the heat and cover with a lid.
- Allow the covered nut mixture to infuse for 3–8 hours. Then strain it through 2 layers of cheesecloth. Discarding the ground almonds.
- Stir the brandy and orange flower water into the syrup.
- Use a small funnel to pour the orgeat into bottles or a jar. Seal and store in the refrigerator for up to 2 weeks.

Falernum

Ingredients:
- ⅓ cup sliced, raw almonds
- 30 whole cloves
- ½ cup of light rum
- 8 limes
- ⅔ cup water
- ½ cup of sugar

Directions:
- Preheat oven to 400°F and toast the almonds on a cookie sheet until slightly darkened (about 5 minutes). Remove sheet and cool.
- Place almonds and cloves in a sealable glass jar and add the rum. Shake and let steep for 2 days.
- Set aside four limes. Zest the remaining limes and add zest to the jar. Shake and let steep for 1 day.
- Strain mix through cheesecloth, pressing to extract as much liquid as possible.
- Juice the four saved limes and strain the juice into a sauce pot.
- Add water and sugar, then bring to a boil on medium heat. Cook until sugar is dissolved (about 5 minutes).
- Let syrup cool, then combine with the strained almond and clove mix.
- If desired, strain mix through a coffee filter. Let it rest for 12 hours before use.

Wine Reduction

The reduction process for white and red wine is basically the same. You are simply combining and boiling wine and sugar to create a soft, sweet wine syrup. These steps combine equal parts wine and sugar (example: 1 cup to 1 cup).

- Measure and add the desired amount of wine into a large saucepan.
- Measure and add an equal amount of raw, unrefined sugar.
- Heat over low heat until low boil occurs, then reduce to a simmer.
- Stirring occasionally, continue heating for 10–15 minutes.
- Remove from heat and cool to room temperature.
- Using funnel, transfer reduction into serving bottles, then refrigerate.

www.ingramcontent.com/pod-product-compliance
Lightning Source LLC
Chambersburg PA
CBHW040846100426
42812CB00014B/2617